THE
HOLY WATER
INCIDENT

About the Author

William Dorian (Nashville, Tennessee) has been interested in the paranormal since the mid-1970s, when—together with Eileen Curran, the daughter of the famous medium Pearl Curran—he began channeling the spirit of Patience Worth. Dorian is a playwright, having written eleven plays (mostly produced) and one screenplay. He is also a theatre director, actor, teacher, and newspaper theatre critic. He has also been a newspaper journalist for over thirty years.

THE
HOLY WATER
INCIDENT

THE TRUE STORY OF A DAUGHTER'S POSSESSION AND EXORCISM

WILLIAM DORIAN

Llewellyn Publications
Woodbury, Minnesota

First Edition
First Printing, 2019

Cover design by Shira Atakpu
Editing by Brian R. Erdrich

Llewellyn Publications is a registered trademark of Llewellyn Worldwide Ltd.

Library of Congress Cataloging-in-Publication Data (Pending)
ISBN: 978-0-7387-6087-2

Llewellyn Publications
A Division of Llewellyn Worldwide Ltd.
2143 Wooddale Drive
Woodbury, MN 55125.2989
www.llewellyn.com

Printed in the United States of America

Dedication

To the memory of Eileen Curran, my early mentor in the paranormal field—and to her muse, Patience Worth, a seventeenth-century storyteller published in the twentieth century whom I hope to meet some day.

To all the unfortunate and suffering individuals and their families who are going through any kind of demonic possession.

Contents

Introduction ... 1

Chapter 1: Patience Worth ... 7

Chapter 2: Our First Haunted House ... 27

Chapter 3: Spiritual Underpinnings ... 39

Chapter 4: The Séance ... 49

Chapter 5: Prelude to the Nightmare ... 59

Chapter 6: The Holy Water Incident ... 63

Chapter 7: The Psych Ward ... 85

Chapter 8: The Exorcism ... 99

Chapter 9: Post Exorcism/Release ... 121

Chapter 10: The Hitchhiking Demon ... 141

Chapter 11: It's Not Over ... 165

Chapter 12: The Voodoo Exorcism ... 177

Chapter 13: Paranormal Incidents Through the Years ... 191

Chapter 14: Life Goes On ... 223

Chapter 15: The Return ... 233

Chapter 16: Spirit Box ... 249

Chapter 17: It Just Keeps Happening ... 259

Chapter 18: The Reboot ... 267

Chapter 19: Possible Explanation ... 283

Conclusion ... 287

Daddy, can you hear me? It's me, Brittany. I'm in this deep, dark place—like a hole, but it's not a hole. I can see you and hear you talking, and I hear them talking with my mouth. They're in my head. My body is moving by itself; I can't control it. I can't speak, but my mouth is talking. I want to talk to you, but they won't let me.

I have to focus on the light. Sometimes when they see the light, they recoil—pull back. But why can't anyone hear me? Wait, I have to be quiet now and still. They're not looking at the light. They're looking at me. They're coming back. They're here. No! Please!

Introduction

The purpose of this book is to recount an incident of demonic possession that afflicted my daughter when she was fifteen. As a result there were harsh, traumatic consequences for her—leaving scars to this day, eighteen years later. Demonic possession, I learned the hard way, is very real. It isn't just mental illness. It happened to my own family, and we weren't hallucinating. My daughter was possessed by demonic entities, period. The incident not only drastically altered her own life, but it also negatively affected the lives of everyone in the immediate family.

I have been a journalist for twenty-five years, so my immediate reaction to my daughter's demonic possession was to keep a detailed journal of what was happening to us. Now, I'm immensely glad that I wrote these bizarre occurrences down while they were going on. If I had waited until later, I'm sure that my rational mind would have convinced me that we had somehow imagined the whole thing or that there was some kind of logical explanation for what was seriously plaguing my family for that initial year, e.g.: "You know, it must have been the wind that moved those items around and rearranged them into neat little stacks; or maybe the floor settling caused all the drawers to open and close by themselves—and then keep banging. Yeah, that's it. Sure, that's all it was."

But luckily I wrote it down when it happened, so I could never be tempted by my rational mind to disregard what my "lying eyes" saw.

It seems curious to me how modern-day Christians base their belief in God, their spirituality, on a book about paranormal/supernatural events that happened thousands of years ago—and yet they deny that paranormal events could possibly be happening today. While they readily accept the premise that Eve talked to Satan and her behavior was influenced by his charisma and abilities of persuasion, they scoff at the notion that Satan and his demons are at work corrupting human beings, stealing souls, and causing very real emotional and physical havoc in contemporary society.

No practicing Christian will deny that Jesus Christ had the divine power to cast out demons. The Gospels are full of incidents depicting him doing just that. But they roll their eyes at the possibility of demonic possession in the twenty-first century (or basically any other paranormal event). They treat anyone who claims to have had an up-close-and-personal experience with a demon as though that individual isn't dealing with a full deck. Jesus cast seven demons out of Mary Magdalene and later sent them into a herd of swine—but that was just in the olden times, right?

With the advent of modern psychology, it's more fashionable today to say that the disciples weren't actually casting out literal demons; they were instead casting out mental illnesses. Really? Are we meant to pick and choose the passages we want to believe and disregard those that seem too fantastic? Sure, if that makes the naysayers sleep better at night ...

After our experiences with demonic possession, I read the Bible cover to cover, front to back, like one would a novel—not just passages plucked from here and there or selected ones referenced by ministers, priests, or rabbis. I wanted to see for myself, so I read it from start to finish, paying particular attention to passages related to demonic possession, angels, miracles, and other paranormal events. Nowhere in the New Testament does it say that once the original apostles, Paul and his disciples, had gone on to their final rewards, the dangers of demonic possession would come to a screeching halt.

The threat of possession by demonic entities is still very real in the modern world, just as it was in the days of Jesus and his apostles. The threat of demons working their evil and trying to influence our lives did not evaporate into thin air after the original Christians passed into the pages of history.

At the time of my daughter's possession, I had been an Episcopalian for twenty-one years (formerly being Roman Catholic). Both my children were baptized into the Episcopal Church, and we had had the same priest most of that time. I truly believed that he was not only our priest but also a close family friend. Apparently I was wrong. When we needed an exorcism, I was unable to obtain one from the Episcopal Church—even though exorcism is an approved rite of that church. As a result of this rejection by my parish priest, I left the Episcopal Church and even Christianity for fifteen years.

But my daughter's possession and our brush with demonic entities and the paranormal merely made me thirst all the more for spiritual answers to the universe. For fifteen years I read everything I could get my hands on, trying to explain what had happened to us. I learned about how Christianity as well as the world's other religions deal with mysticism and the unexplained. But more relevant to this book, I learned about the paranormal—which simply means "beyond the accepted norm."

After all my studies, I cannot say with any certainty that I know exactly what demonic entities are, precisely where they come from, or exactly why they feel compelled to torment mankind. But I have theories and I have learned to deal with the paranormal experiences that plagued my family for many years.

This book is also, and perhaps most importantly, a spiritual journey—a journey away from God and then full cycle back to his grace. As my daughter and I did battle with demonic entities and tried to deal with the destruction left in our lives, we concurrently went on a spiritual journey—though we veered far from it for a decade and a half. I returned to Christianity, albeit with numerous other influences. My daughter, however, is still searching for the exact metaphysical format that will give her spiritual satisfaction.

This book is not primarily about returning to religion. I'm not here to preach, and I won't be quoting scriptures. The book is primarily about the paranormal occurrences that turned our family upside down so many years ago. Things happened in our home that I know will be hard for most people to believe. Even at the time, I knew these things would be difficult for *me* to believe later if I didn't write them down immediately. So being a newspaper reporter and editor, the natural thing for me to do was to keep a detailed journal. That's what I did in 2001 as it all transpired. I knew that if I didn't, my logical, rational mind would convince me later that it either hadn't happened at all or, perhaps, it wasn't as bad as I had initially thought.

But even though I kept a journal of our paranormal events in 2001, I couldn't bring myself to go any further with it for many years. Frankly, it was too traumatic a subject for me to process for a very long time. I told myself that someday I would turn that journal into a book—with the goal being to help others who might be having similar paranormal disruptions in their lives.

Meanwhile, I continued to write for a newspaper and also penned eleven plays and one screenplay. My educational background is in theatre, and I taught theatre at two universities and in other schools over the years. I continued to direct and act in plays and produced the plays I wrote here in Nashville. But the journal of our paranormal brush with the demonic languished on my computer. Then one day, out of the blue I suppose, I just decided it was time to write the book.

I think that my decision to finally finish the story had a great deal to do with the spiritual awakening I was going through—partially because of years of reading about the paranormal and partially because of personal spiritual revelations. But my spiritual rebirth is only a very small part of this story.

I feel it is now my mission in life to help anyone else who might be going through what we went through in our battle with demonic entities in 2001 and since. Not only does the fallout of these events still affect my daughter and our family today, eighteen years later, but paranormal episodes still happen occasionally in my home and to my daughter. Some of these post-possession events are described later in the book.

I have finally reconciled with my Christian heritage and returned to the Episcopal Church. The priest who turned me down for an exorcism was acting out of his own fear—and not official Episcopal Church policy or proper procedure.

Chapter 1
Patience Worth

Before I can recount the story of my daughter's possession by demonic entities in 2001, I need to take you back to New Orleans circa 1974. It was there that I met the spirit of a Puritan woman named Patience Worth who had died over three hundred years earlier. The Patience Worth/Pearl Curran phenomenon may very well have been the most famous paranormal/literary case of the early twentieth century. I became involved when I became a friend of the Curran family. This was my first real experience with the paranormal.

I was a graduate student at the University of New Orleans and living in the married dorms with my first wife. I was in the master's program in theatre, but I was about to be exposed to a universe and spiritual construct that had nothing to do with acting and directing. Though I had been very interested in what most folks called "the supernatural" back then ever since I was a kid, I'd never had any real experience with the paranormal. Spooky movies, ghost stories, and reading a few books on the subject hadn't prepared me for what I was about to encounter. From a spiritual and metaphysical standpoint, my life was about to be irreversibly changed—although the process would still take over thirty more years.

My wife Sherree and I had become friends with the couple who lived next door to us in the dorm. Ronny was an undergrad student and his wife Joan worked as a secretary. During a conversation over dinner one evening, I off-handedly mentioned my interest in the paranormal. We'd been talking about a paper I'd just written for a film class I was taking where I compared the novel *The Exorcist* to the recently released movie version. Then Joan mentioned that Ronny had an aunt, Eileen, whose mother had been an internationally famous psychic back in the early twentieth century. She suggested that I might be interested in meeting Eileen. Any break from reading books about Stanislavsky's acting theories or seventeenth-century costumes, modes, and manners sounded like a worthwhile diversion to me—so I enthusiastically agreed.

We all got together one Sunday afternoon in the spring of 1974. The atmosphere of my first encounter with the spirit of Patience Worth was imminently un-spooky and non-supernatural. In broad daylight, with no flickering candles and the TV droning in the next room, Sherree and I were introduced to Eileen, a perky and intelligent woman in her fifties. Eileen was an artist (a talented painter) with a wry sense of humor and an intense curiosity about all things spiritual and metaphysical. She described to me how her mother, Pearl Curran, had been a prominent psychic, channeling the spirit of Patience Worth for twenty-four years. Pearl first contacted the spirit of Patience over the Ouija board in 1913. It started as a game, a lark, when Pearl and a friend asked questions of the board as they lightly touched the planchette with their fingers. It didn't take long for the two women to start getting answers, with neither of them feeling they were the source of the planchette's movement. Patience communicated in perfect Early Modern English (the language of Shakespeare and the King James Bible). During that time, Patience authored six novels, several books of poetry, and two plays. Her work was acclaimed by critics and sold quite well.

Pearl was a housewife who never went to college and should have had no knowledge of Early Modern English. However, her writings were analyzed by linguistics experts of the day who concluded the syntax and structure was indeed genuine and authentic to the early 1600s. Patience claimed she had always wanted to be a storyteller during her time on earth but was not given the education. Using Pearl as her medium, Patience intended to fulfill her dream.

Eileen told me that at first the women would have to stop frequently to write down the board's communications. Sometimes Pearl's husband would act as scribe to speed things along, but even that was a slow and tedious process. But then after several months of meticulously taking Patience's dictation via the Ouija board, Pearl switched to automatic writing—almost mindlessly letting her pen go wherever it wanted without her conscious participation. She would usually start by simply making doodles with her pen. The trick, Eileen said, was to let your mind go blank while doodling. Eventually, the doodles became words and sentences—but even then, it was important to keep your mind blank.

Pearl could actually have a conversation with you about a totally unrelated subject at the same time Patience was guiding the more modern woman's pen, weaving tales set centuries earlier.

To help me catch up on the saga of Patience Worth / Pearl Curran, Eileen recommended I read a book that had just been published about her mother and her adventures with Patience. She said *Singer in the Shadows* by Irving Litvag was the most current, up-to-date, authoritative book on the subject. There were also a number of older books written about the verbose, red-haired Puritan and her twentieth-century secretary, both by literary scholars and parapsychologists. I hurried out to a bookstore the next day and scooped up a copy, which I found to be quite well written and highly informative.

As I poured over Litvag's fascinating story about Pearl and Patience, the part that really caught my attention was concerned with a prophesy about the psychic abilities of Pearl's daughter, Eileen. Like many children, Eileen rebelled against the lifestyle of her parent and was determined to have absolutely nothing to do with anything paranormal. However, Litvag mentioned that Patience had predicted that, after Pearl died, she would be able to continue her writing through Eileen. I saw that as an important point, a eureka moment, in fact. Oddly, it was something Eileen hadn't bothered to mention to me at our meeting. Naturally, I got on the phone and set up another meeting with Eileen. She was familiar with the prophecy of her psychic gifts but had never taken any of that seriously. However, she humored me and said she'd be willing to give it a try.

The next day I rushed off to a Woolworth's and paid about four dollars for a Parker Brothers Ouija board. Sherree, Joan, and I met with Eileen and her teenaged daughter, Tara, at their apartment in Metairie, a suburb of New Orleans. Eileen's husband, Ron, an artist himself who made his living as a bartender in the French Quarter, was at work. Although a jovial enough guy, Ron wasn't much interested in the Patience Worth lore. Eileen was friendly and talkative but obviously nervous about testing the theory she might pick up where her mother left off way back in 1937.

Again, there were no spooky, dimly flickering candles. Bored with the whole affair, Tara watched TV nearby as Eileen and I touched our fingers to the planchette on the Ouija board. Although I hadn't expected any immediate response, the planchette rapidly danced about the board in all directions—more than a bit hard to keep up with. It didn't spell anything out initially, but rather seemed simply to be getting its bearings or flexing its muscles as it dashed frantically across the board. Naturally, Eileen and I both disavowed instigating the motion. After a while, it slowed down and went repeatedly from the P to the W—back and forth, back and forth. Excitedly, I asked if we had contacted Patience. The reply follows:

"A wench I was, a wench I am. Patience Worth, my name."

Eileen asked, rather skeptically, "Why come to me now after all these years?"

Without hesitation, the board spelled out: "My harp hath never left thee. P. W., P. W. Grasp a hope, hold a thought. Thee, I see. P. W."

To see if the entity would communicate with anyone else, Eileen and I turned over the planchette to Sherree and Joan. Now the entity seemed to struggle, and the planchette moved much more slowly from letter to letter. However, finally it spelled out: "Leave thee alone. Leave thee alone. Now quit. The tabby sleepeth. P. W."

We took that to mean that Patience would rather talk to Eileen and I, so we switched back, asking why Patience preferred to communicate with us. Patience quickly replied:

"All grapes grow slow 'pon the vine. Sting not the bud afore it blooms, P. W."

Eileen then inquired about her daughter, Tara. Apparently, the typical teen angst had reared its ugly head in their mother-daughter relationship.

"She doth love thee weel but fears for thee and knoweth not why. P. W."

Eileen then asked why (after all these years) Patience had decided to start communicating again.

"No rappin' 'pon the gate, and thee doth hold the rust o' time. Now the need, the need. P. W."

It was getting late, and I could sense that everyone but Eileen and I was getting a little sleepy, so I told Patience we'd see her again soon.

"Aye, take thy hearts wi' thy loves, P. W."

And that's how it all started.

Although Eileen took our communications with a woman who had been dead for three hundred years in stride, I was beside myself. She'd never personally chatted with Patience before, but she'd grown up with her. It was all old hat to Eileen. But to me, all this paranormal stuff was simply astounding. I was ready to jump in with both feet. I wanted to do more sessions. I started keeping a journal. I wrote everything down. I even wrote the author of *Singer in the Shadows* a letter telling him all about Eileen and our experiences.

But, of course, Eileen regarded the incident much more calmly. In fact, regardless of the evidence of Patience's existence that we were getting over the Ouija board, she was keeping everything at arm's length. She had resisted the idea of psychic phenomena throughout her childhood, for the same reason many children resist being like their parents. Peer pressure. The other kids she knew at school had parents who went to work, went to church, maybe worked in the yard or puttered around the house. They weren't internationally famous psychics touring the world, lecturing, giving demonstrations, or writing books that were reviewed by famous critics. The entire Patience Worth episode had truly been Eileen's own Puritan dilemma.

Now, even though she had separated herself from her mother's notoriety, Eileen had become more and more interested in spiritual matters, ESP, PSI, psychic phenomena, etc. As they say, "The acorn doesn't fall far from the tree"—even though Eileen had repeatedly asserted that she wanted nothing to do with her mother's otherworldly lifestyle.

Pearl Curran was a household name during the 1920s amongst both metaphysical devotees and the literary intelligentsia. But Eileen hadn't shared her mother's limelight, and life hadn't been particularly kind. She was a trained and talented visual artist, but by the time I met her, she had mostly given up on her art and had become a bit of a recluse. Ron was her third husband and was over a decade younger than Eileen—and not especially supportive of his wife's superior talent. He was also an astrologer and helped make ends meet by doing astrological charts and paintings.

(Ron even did an astrological chart on me, which supposedly indicated I had considerable psychic abilities myself. That came as a complete surprise, because at the ripe age of twenty-three, I had never had any kind of psychic experiences. With age, for better or worse, that would change.)

Eileen's daughter, Tara, was the bright spot in an otherwise rather dismal existence. She was a pretty typical teenager who didn't want to be too closely associated with her mom, but any time the subject of Tara came up, Eileen's eyes always sparkled.

I was totally fired up by our encounters with Patience, and our contact with this long-deceased Puritan seemed to be giving Eileen new hope for her future—perhaps the first in quite a long time.

School at the university was just about to let out for the summer, so I would be having nearly three months off to basically hold sessions with Eileen/Patience, do research on Patience, and begin writing a book about our experiences.

The information we were getting from Patience started snowballing. She began writing poems again, as well as an autobiography of herself as a little girl. Once you adjust to the archaic English, Patience's prose is quite engaging. Here's a sample from her autobiography:

And I, too, would ha'e wings to soar. I, too, ha'e a song to sing, but dames sing not here in this time. Red, red is the sky, and late the hour. And still he waits [her father]. Home not shall I go. But where, where to go? Now the grasses are dampin' my hem, and crushed is the bonnet flung down from the head.

"Patience, Patience!" I hear, I hear, and I do not heed. And the hour passes, and then another hour. "Patience, Patience!"

Tis closer ... The step is 'pon the stone, and the grass rustles. The shadow looms, and I make me small and tremble.

"Ye urchin thing, ye strange creature art! Thou art not woman; thou art not man. Thou art a stranger to this land. What ails thee? What sic thing possesses thee?

"... What will be when to the home we return? What dark silence will lie between us like the sullen night?"

After forty years, Patience was writing again.

Within a few weeks, the planchette was moving so quickly across the Ouija board that we could barely keep up with it. Plus, there was always the drawback of having Sherree, Joan, or someone transcribe what was being received—and as I've mentioned, they weren't as enthusiastic about the whole endeavor as Eileen and I.

We discovered that Eileen could chat with Patience via the Ouija board without anyone else touching the planchette. However, she didn't like this method, saying it just made her "feel silly."

After about a month of these sessions, Eileen suggested we try a different method. She wanted to try the automatic writing her mother had started using after Patience proved so prolific. While terribly exciting, the Ouija board is a cumbersome method of communication. It may score high for atmosphere and ambiance, but it is painfully, frustratingly slow. One day Eileen got out a legal pad and a pen and started making doodle-like drawings that after a while turned into horizontal scribbles that eventually turned into words. Sometimes she actually looked at what she was writing, but just as often she stared out into space as she wrote.

Most of the material we got that summer from Patience was communicated via Eileen's automatic writing. However, occasionally we would revert back to the Ouija board—especially if I specifically had a question for Patience.

I've always been interested in theories about God, ultimate reality, religion, and metaphysics. Since Patience was speaking to us from the other side, I hoped she would be in a position to shed some light on the true makeup of the universe. Based on her published writings via Pearl Curran, I knew Patience was very religious. One evening I asked about the truth concerning God or an ultimate creator. Her personal views on spirituality were surprisingly liberal and open-minded for someone supposedly brought up in the strict, fundamentalist Puritan religion, for example:

PW: "…each way be a river that leadeth to the sea, and the sea takes all things unto it. So then take what river thou wilt, what way thou wilt. They all lead to the sea. If not, find then thin ain river. For each o' us there be one. I am that I am; thou art what thou art. The word is what thou seeth athin the word. He is the word, an' what is o' him is the word…It is the quest o' the seeker that maketh the holy path."

A couple of times Sherree and I went back to Nashville for weekend visits, Ouija board in tow. Patience would still come through with Sherree and I manning the planchette, while my mother took dictation. We'd chat with Patience about insignificant things just to keep in practice. But even though Eileen wasn't present, Patience's style was consistent with the material we'd received with Eileen—friendly and humorous Early Modern English.

Once during one of these sessions without Eileen, Patience predicted the coming demise of my marriage with Sherree:

"A tabby sleepeth beneath thy feet. [Patience often identified herself as a tabby.] The trees are green with the feel o' spring, but thy heart is burdened because, as with spring fever, a love thy desire. Thy art not very sure, but thou art true."

Sherree and I had not been getting along well for some time, and the marriage would only last another six months or so. Sherree returned to Tennessee, and I remained in New Orleans. Unhappy with the curriculum at the University of New Orleans, I transferred to Tulane University, where I finished my master's in theatre.

My relationship with Eileen/Patience continued throughout my stay at Tulane, and I wrote a book about our experiences with the Puritan woman during two summers off from school. A small publisher accepted my work, and of course I was elated. However, life throws you curveballs sometimes. The publisher wanted to see Eileen and me pen a whole series of books by Patience. But by this time, Eileen's husband had had enough of this metaphysical nonsense. Ron put his foot down and forbade Eileen's participation in further contacts with Patience.

When the publisher learned there would only be one Patience Worth book, the project was shelved. Naturally, I was devastated. I planned to make my living in theatre, but I didn't want to say goodbye to either Eileen or Patience. But Eileen was totally subservient to her husband. Although they were both artists and had lived a Bohemian lifestyle in the French Quarter before Tara came along, Eileen always let Ron run the show. He said no, and that was that. There was no book, and I never saw Eileen again after 1975.

I called Eileen five or six years later just to catch up with her and fill her in on how my life was going. Ron answered the phone and told me that Eileen had died only a couple of years after I'd last seen her. I was shocked because she was only in her fifties and seemed to me to be in good health. I pressed him for details, but he only volunteered that she had not been in good health for some time. To this day, I consider Eileen to have been one of the most influential people in my life.

But that wasn't the last I would hear of Patience Worth. During one of Eileen's early automatic writing sessions, Patience had told me that she would be able to communicate with me directly without Eileen.

PW: "I am close with thee, Will [she always called me Will], an' shall not leave thee, e'en if there should be a time where thou thinketh I ha'e gone."

I continued to chat with Patience off and on for years whenever I'd get out my old Woolworth's Ouija board. I never knew what she was going to say, but it was always relatively easy for me to dial up her frequency. It was just a game for many years, and I must admit the Ouija board can be a great pastime at parties. Once during a theatre cast party that had included a bit too much drinking, we'd pulled out Ouija and asked Patience to connect us to William Shakespeare. Here's our reply:

PW: "Thou wouldst speak unto Will Shakespeare? He'd ha'e none o' that. There be an unkindness here, Will. Tis o' the cup, Will, the cup. There be sickness in't. An' foul wou'd I be to beg o' him a presence. Thou art not o' a comfort o' this, Will. Yea, I know it."

It's true. I thought some of the drinking had gotten out of hand, and I wanted them to take this exercise more seriously.

During another communication, I asked Patience to give me a glimpse of my future—particularly pertaining to my own personal psychic development.

PW: "Trust thou in me and follow me 'pon the path. Wouldst thee find a sticky moss underneath the pebbles, I'd be wi' thee. Aye, now tis dark, dark, dark an' more. I'll say me more anon. But now tis dark past lightin' o' it. Anon, Will."

Patience's words seemed unclear and somewhat disjointed at the time. However many years later, I would take great comfort from them—making me quite glad I'd always painstakingly written all her utterances down.

Over the next ten years or so, my waking efforts were mostly concentrated on making a living and not chatting with spirits. Nevertheless, I'd occasionally pursue the odd foray into the world of the Ouija board. I saw it as an interesting but harmless game. Later, in the hands of my teenaged daughter, it would take on a more ominous tone.

Patience, the Bell Witch, Zoroaster, and a Prophesy

I had a musician friend named Dan who enjoyed talking to the spirits. Dan and I wrote songs together and sometimes after an evening of writing, singing, and playing guitars, we'd sit down and crank up the Ouija board. Patience was often eager to talk—as well as a rather motley crew of other spirits. Dan had recently been doing some reading about the ancient religion of Zoroastrianism, and sometimes we'd ask for and receive communications with Zoroaster. The messages usually paralleled Zoroaster's philosophy of a universal struggle between the forces of light and the forces of evil, so it might have actually been old Zoroaster himself—or it might just as well have been Dan's subconscious.

Since Dan and I both grew up in Robertson County, Tennessee (adjacent to Metro Nashville/Davidson County), we were both fascinated with the legend of the Bell Witch—probably the most famous case of poltergeist activity in the history of the United States. The Bell Witch (usually referred to as Kate) haunted the Bell farm in Adams, Tennessee, around 1820—about thirty-five miles from where Dan and I grew up in Greenbrier. The so-called "witch" (actually a spirit manifestation capable of moving physical objects, and capable of clearly audible, highly literate speech) is credited with killing John Bell, Sr.—the only case in American history wherein a spirit is truly credited with murder.

There are many theories as to what exactly Kate was: a demon; an elemental nature spirit; the ghost of a Native American; or even possibly poltergeist manifestations caused by the subconscious psychic abilities of John Bell's thirteen-year-old daughter, Betsy. But whatever the spirit was, 150 years after its brush with infamy in Adams, Tennessee, it (or something claiming to be it) visited me and Dan one evening.

On that occasion, "Kate" seemed eager to talk to Dan and me on the Ouija board. We'd chatted with Patience for a bit, and then Dan asked to speak to Kate. The communication we got was preceded by voluminous profanities and numerous threats. Then a friendlier spirit dropped in.

New Spirit: "I'll protect thee from Kate. I owe ye that."

I assumed this was Patience, although I didn't think she owed me anything. So I asked if this new voice was she. It said, "No." So I asked to whom we were speaking.

New Spirit: "Zoroaster. We ha'e been friends o'er the ages—afore and anon. So tonight, go in peace. But I'll not always be wi' thee. Take care o' the wee one."

I tried to get some clarification on that last bit, since I had no children at the time. There was no "wee one" in my life.

New Spirit: "Twenty-five years o' thy clock. I see it. Look to thy guard o' the wee one."

That was all the board had to say—no further clarifications. This new spirit (Zoroaster?) seemed to be predicting something, but I didn't have the foggiest idea what.

Dan and I were both a bit shaken and decided to call it a night. He lived in an isolated farmhouse on a gravel road, so the thoughts of driving home alone weren't exactly appealing. But Zoroaster must have ridden shotgun with me as my old VW Beetle chugged along through the night, with neither the Bell Witch nor any other entities bothering me on that lonely country lane.

The entire incident was soon forgotten and would remain so for nearly three decades. When getting messages over the Ouija board, we were usually very careful to write everything down. I kept these communications in a box with all the Patience Worth material I had accumulated. And though I moved numerous times over the years, I kept that box—not because of the various messages from the spiritual "nits" or "ithers" as Patience called them, but because I sensed that Patience Worth's material was important. Even if I hadn't been able to publish the book, I still felt that my connections with Patience were significant (including the "nits" and "ithers").

I only just stumbled across the notes I had kept of my Ouija board adventures all those years ago as I was preparing for this material about Brittany's possession. I see now that there was definitely a connection, and I'm glad I lugged the box around all this time. "I'll not always be wi' thee. Take care o' the wee one" now seems an ominous foreboding of things to come.

Patience Peeks over My Shoulder as I Take Care of Business

Eventually I remarried and, naturally, had to be preoccupied with making a living. Dan and I were never able to sell a song, but over the years I did a bit of everything, including shelving books in the public library; selling cars; teaching high school English, speech, and theatre; teaching theatre in several universities; and finally working as a newspaper reporter, editor, and columnist—all the while doing lots of acting and directing in community theatre.

All the while, I retained my interest in the paranormal. But it was mostly limited to reading books or watching movies and the occasional documentary.

In 1979, I moved about thirty miles outside of Nashville to the rural county seat of Lebanon, Tennessee. I had secured a job teaching at Cumberland College (soon to become a university). By this time, I was married to my second wife, Linda—an intelligent and urbane woman who had grown up mostly in Europe where her father had been stationed at various army bases.

Linda had no interest in the paranormal, aside from being a fan of Stephen King novels. But she was well aware of my interest in it. My friend Dan came over often and she indulged our dalliances with the Ouija board, but she had no curiosity into the information we were receiving.

I taught at Cumberland for a year, then landed a gig teaching English, theatre, and speech at Lebanon High School (which paid a bit more money). I also became involved in the local Sound & Light community theatre group, so life became quite busy. There just wasn't much time for paranormal explorations or speculations. Occasionally, Dan and I dusted off the Ouija and talked to Patience and the "ithers," but that was about it on the paranormal front.

I only taught high school the one year. Moving to secondary education proved to be a mistake. I far preferred the subject matter–based teaching found at the university level to the disciple-based teaching on the high school level.

After the high school debacle, I worked about a year with a Tennessee-based film production company attempting to make a movie about the Bell Witch legend. They had a pretty good screenplay and we came close to making it happen, but close doesn't win the cigar. It wasn't meant to be. When my paychecks stopped coming, I had to give up the project.

Marriage number two was also crumbling by this point. Linda and I lacked core common interests, and we grew further and further apart. She had no interest in theatre or the paranormal. There were also personal issues intervening, and before long we divorced.

After a while, I had reconnected with a former fellow teacher from my high school teaching days, Sheila Massey, when we were in a play together. Finally, a woman who shared my passion for theatre! We did countless plays together, and she had a passing interest in the paranormal. We fell in love, dated for five years, and got married by my uncle who was a county magistrate in Robertson County.

After the failed Bell Witch movie venture, I tried my hand at being a social worker for the state of Tennessee for a couple of years. I found the work ultimately too depressing but am most proud of having rescued several small children from physically and sexually abusive parents.

During rehearsals for a play I was in, I became friends with a gentleman named Jack. A successful entrepreneur, Jack was starting a public relations firm and asked me to come work for him as a copywriter. I jumped at the chance to earn money as a writer and worked at his firm for about three years until it finally fizzled. The small town just hadn't grown to the point where it could support its own PR firm. However, I enjoyed the work, the chance to know Jack (one of life's *real* characters)—and, perhaps most importantly, my work with the county historian, which taught me tons about researching Victorian homes, including the home where I saw my first ghost.

Editing a Paranormal Magazine

About this time, I also became friends with a local psychic named Carol who did readings in a nearby town. I had written a freelance newspaper article about her when she published a book about ESP and her experiences with psychic phenomena. Carol wanted to start publishing a monthly newsletter/magazine about the people involved with psychic phenomena in the Nashville area. Nowadays there is an active community of psychics, paranormal investigators, Pagans, pantheists, metaphysical seekers of all kinds, you name it, in the Music City area. But back then, this community was just beginning to come out of the closet. There were actually quite few who would admit to being interested in metaphysical or psychic subjects. But New Age thought was slowly becoming more accepted by the mid-eighties, and Carol felt there would be a market for her newsletter. She wanted me to be the editor. I would be a one-man-show. I'd do all the interviews, write all the stories, do the layouts, and arrange for a printing company to publish it.

I interviewed numerous local psychics, a very metaphysical Unity minister, and several nationally known psychics who came through Nashville. I even did a phone interview with Uri Geller, the Israeli psychic who's internationally famous for bending small metal objects with his mind. One local psychic I got to know was Laurel. Laurel had already had a career as a writer and by then was middle-aged. But she decided to leave her boring job with a publishing company and "put her shingle out" to go into full-time work as a medium/psychic. I learned later that Laurel had inherited her ability from her mother, who had also been a writer and one of the few female war correspondents during World War II. She had dallied in ESP games with her mom as a little girl, but the gift within her had mushroomed by the time I met her. Now she was ready to take it to a whole different level. I mention Laurel here because she plays a very important role in my daughter's exorcism-to-come, which would change all our lives within another decade and a half.

I absolutely loved my job as editor of Carol's monthly metaphysical newsletter, but we were only able to come out with a few issues. Publishing a monthly periodical proved considerably more expensive than Carol had anticipated, and we were forced to close our little operation down before it had a chance to catch on.

Chapter 2
Our First Haunted House

There were no more firsthand experiences with the paranormal until my daughter, Brittany, was born in 1985. We were living in an old Victorian two-story home on Greenwood Street by then. By that time, I was working the night shift as a reporter for a daily newspaper in Lebanon. During the day, I taught a couple of adjunct classes in theatre at Cumberland University. I would come in from the newspaper about daybreak, sleep until noon, then tumble out of bed, eat, shower and get to Cumberland for my first class at two p.m. The house I lived in with Sheila and our toddler daughter was about a block from the campus. Later research revealed the house had been built in 1901 to serve as a home for the college president, though it hadn't been owned by Cumberland in many years.

More recently, it had been owned by the same family for forty years or so. The next-door neighbor (an elderly lady who had lived there since the flapper days) told me a brother and sister had resided there for decades. I never knew if they died in the house or not, but I wouldn't be surprised. People didn't rush off to the hospital every time they got a sniffle (or even had chest pains) back in the day. The house had undergone an amateur restoration in the early seventies, but by the time I bought it in 1985, it needed quite a bit more work. I purchased it from the family who had remodeled it, but Sheila and I still had to spend lots of money on it just for regular maintenance. It had been vacant for at least five years when we moved in, so it took months just to get it livable. Unforeseen money and tons of elbow grease were needed, but we still loved that old house. It felt like a comfy old slipper.

I definitely would not call our house on Greenwood Street haunted—no more so than any eighty-year-old house. My research did not reveal any particularly traumatic events happening there. People may have died in the house, but that was pretty much the norm back then.

My experiences with the house were all pleasant, but we did have a few unthreatening paranormal experiences there. Often when we pulled into the driveway with Brittany strapped into her child carrier in the backseat, she would point to someone we couldn't see, saying: "There's my lady." This happened numerous times, and there was never anyone there. It seemed a bit odd, but we never made a big deal out of it—and within a minute or two, Brittany's attention would always be diverted to something else important, like a passing butterfly or a doll that required immediate attention. Like most parents, we chalked the lady up to an imaginary playmate.

Brittany's lady was a part of her play ritual inside the house as well. She often sat at a toddler-sized plastic table and had tea parties with her dolls. Sheila and I were frequently active participants in the tea parties, but if Britt was alone with her dolls you could hear her chattering away to her invisible guests. If asked to whom she was talking, the answer was invariably "my lady." She also liked to sit on the steps going to the upstairs bedrooms and play with her toys, animatedly making up conversations for her various stuffed and plastic friends.

One night when I was at work at the newspaper, Sheila looked up to see Brittany leaving her toys behind on the lower steps and cheerily toddling eight or nine steps higher than we liked her to go, apparently in pursuit of something Sheila couldn't see. She snatched the toddler up and brought her back downstairs, with Brittany protesting that she needed to follow her lady. After that incident, we put a removable wooden gate across the stairs so Britt couldn't venture up more than a few steps. But this was nothing more than many parents go through trying to keep their young children from falling down the stairs.

I had become good friends with Laurel, the psychic I met while I was editing the paranormal newsletter. Every six or eight months, I'd go to Laurel for a personal psychic reading. I even took Brittany with me on several occasions. Laurel was very fond of Brittany and told me she felt that my daughter would prove to have psychic abilities of her own—perhaps even acting as a psychic/medium herself someday. When I mentioned Brittany's lady to Laurel, she said this was nothing to worry about and that she felt this was a "protective spirit" who had my daughter's best interests at heart.

I frankly never took Brittany's lady too seriously until I met her myself. After working all night at the newspaper and getting my usual six hours sleep, my alarm went off. Time to get ready to teach my classes. As I reached over to turn the blaring alarm off, I was mystified to see a woman standing at the foot of my bed. I'll never forget the image I saw—a middle-aged woman with short, light brown, bobbed hair, dressed circa 1940s in a tan skirt and burgundy sweater. Her outline was crisp, and the coloring of my curious new friend was sharp. However, she was transparent. Her features were perfectly clear, but I was a bit unnerved that I could also see through her. She had a kind smile on her face, as if amused by my reaction to her. I only saw her for a minute, but there was no question in my mind that she was real.

All my life, I had figured if I ever saw a ghost, I would be paralyzed with fear. But the experience wasn't scary at all. My immediate reaction was one of interest and fascination.

I was so fascinated by what I had seen, I told my students when I got to the college. Interestingly enough, no one seemed to think I was insane and we spent a few minutes just talking about ghosts in general. Quite a few of them even had their own personal stories to share. Even back in 1987, it was amazing how many people would admit to having seen a spirit.

This was my first episode of seeing a ghost, but it made me remember some of the stories my mother had told me about her spirit encounters. At her apartment in Nashville, she used to see the transparent ghost of an African American man standing outside her bedroom in the hall. She was so shaken by her first sighting of the apparition that she called me knowing I had had spiritual experiences with Eileen/Patience and would be sympathetic. The next time we got together, she admitted to me that she had seen spirits on a very irregular basis all her life.

But anything supernatural or occult truly frightened my mom, and she didn't like to talk about it. She told me that when the original Boris Karloff movie *Frankenstein* came out back in 1931, she went to the theatre with her two brothers to see it—not really knowing what the movie was about. She was so terrified, she jumped up from her seat and ran out of the theatre, leaving her brothers sitting in the theatre alone. They ribbed her for her lack of courage on into adulthood. Mom never mentioned seeing ghosts to me again, but seeing Brittany's lady myself made me start wondering then if the ability to see them, even occasionally, might be hereditary.

After we'd lived in the Victorian house on Greenwood Street about five years, I got a job as editor of a small-town weekly newspaper in the adjacent town of Mt. Juliet. We sold the house when Brittany was four and moved so I could be closer to work. I hated leaving the house on Greenwood, but I felt that if I was going to edit Mt. Juliet's newspaper, I needed to be a part of the community. We moved into a small, modern, brick house in a subdivision near a lake. Brittany loved to go down to the shallow creek behind the house and play with two of the neighborhood kids about her age. She was known to bring several slimy, creepy, swishy little critters the kids found in the creek up to the house as presents. The little house was peaceful and serene—a pretty typical slice of Americana.

Past Life Memories

Our year spent in the creek house saw no paranormal apparitions or manifestations of any kind. Brittany never mentioned seeing her lady and I certainly never saw her again, so I concluded she was attached to the house on Greenwood. However, I did experience one metaphysical event while we lived in the house by the creek.

After Sheila, Brittany, and I had gone to bed one evening, I awoke in the middle of the night after an extremely vivid nightmare. I never had a dream like it before or since. The dream/ nightmare was set in pre-World War II Nazi Germany. I was in the dream, but I was very different than I am now. I could feel deep inside that this was *me*, but I didn't look anything at all like I did, at the time, in 1989. I have dark brown, curly hair and gray eyes. My features are kind of Mediterranean with a Roman-type nose that dominates my face—like it's the first thing to enter the room. I've had a number of people tell me I look Jewish even though I have no Jewish heritage. But in the dream, I was blond and very fair-skinned with deep, translucent blue eyes. The only similarity was that I was very light of frame, just as I really am. In the dream, I was a radio announcer and I was broadcasting a message that was very anti-Adolf Hitler. Perhaps this was right before Hitler became chancellor of Germany, because I can't imagine my anti-Hitler news would have cleared the censors after his ascension to power. In the middle of my broadcast, four or five of Hitler's Brown Shirt thugs burst into the sound room, snatched the microphone out of my hand, beat the holy hell out of me, and carried me off to what seemed to be some kind of prison where I was severely tortured, abused, and generally mutilated. I was in the middle of one of many torture sessions when I abruptly woke up in a cold sweat, shaking.

I quickly sat up in bed and frantically looked around the room in every direction. I was stunned to find myself back in our bedroom; I was so certain that the dream was really happening. Sheila was sound asleep, and I didn't bother her. I got up and went to the bathroom. Turning the sink's faucet on, I splashed water in my face hoping this might bring me back to reality. What happened next has haunted me ever since. Staring back at me was the face of the blond radio announcer. I knew the dream was over—the cold water saw to that. But the face that was looking back at me was not my own. It was unmistakably the face of the man I had been dreaming was me. Although I was quite literally terrified, I was also fascinated and continued to gaze into the mirror for several seconds.

I felt empathy and compassion for what he had been through—because I had somehow experienced it myself. I looked slightly down toward the sink while all the while still keeping the vision of this blond, blue-eyed intruder in my line of vision. As I looked down, he did the same. It was truly as if this reflection was me—except it looked altogether like someone else. I looked toward the door and yelled for Sheila. When I looked back in the mirror, my reflection had reassumed my normal features. I was me again, albeit sweaty and still shaking. I went back into the bedroom and found Sheila still sleeping away. She's not easily awakened; my shriek had certainly proved insufficient. I went back to bed, but I'm not sure I ever went back to sleep that night. This episode rattled me to such an extent that I didn't sleep really well for months. I couldn't get the images of that blond, blue-eyed "me-but-not-me" out of my head. The memories I had of the abuse and torture he suffered were so intense for several months it actually made concentrating very difficult.

I never had another nightmare about this unfortunate man whose memories I shared, and it took me a very long time to get him out of my head. Was this an experience of a past life remembered? I had believed in reincarnation since my first encounters with Eileen in New Orleans. Living multiple lives in order to perfect your soul is both more logical and more compassionate than believing in a God who would condemn you to eternal damnation after only one lifetime.

I told my psychic adviser, Laurel, about the dream/nightmare (and subsequent vision in the mirror), and she was certain I had had a past-life memory. She further explained that many believe that time is actually an illusion and is only a convenient way for our simple minds to understand the expansion of the universe. If this is true and all time happens simultaneously, then for one brief moment I became a blond radio announcer in Nazi Germany, and he may have become a newspaper editor in our time frame.

But the most relevant aspect of this experience, as pertains to my daughter Brittany, perhaps had more to do with genes than a discussion of reincarnation. I had told Laurel about my mom's lifelong, sporadic experiences seeing apparitions, as well as my own single encounter with a ghost. When she first met Brittany as a toddler, she had sensed that Britt had a special aura about her—a propensity for future psychic abilities.

"Your mom saw apparitions," she said. "You saw the one spirit and had the reincarnational dream, and Brittany is very psychic. I'd have to conclude it's hereditary." Maybe she was right, but at the time I felt about as psychic as an old sock. I was more concerned with editing the newspaper and maybe learning lines to plays.

But her words did make me think, especially later in life, when I began having precognitive dreams on a fairly regular basis. I often dream about people I don't know or about situations to which I have no connection in the present. The dreams are always much more vivid than regular dreams, and I always remember them in great detail upon awakening. Then later that day or perhaps later that week, I will meet that person or end up in that certain place I'd dreamed about. Also, the people and situations are never very important, and I have no control over the dreams. I can't ask to dream about winning the lottery and expect to see a ticket with the winning numbers. I suppose these precognitive dreams have a connection to the theory that all time happens at once. Just the fact that I have them at all, and that they come true, could be a genetic clue to the abilities I would see later in my daughter.

For a brief moment, I connected to my blond Nazi-era doppelganger. I experienced his life and felt his pain, and he probably experienced my life and perceived my reality in some way. But regardless of the machinations of how this quantum, interdimensional ballet may have played out, I have been firmly convinced ever since in the reality of reincarnation and in the psychic gene that might link our family.

Life Trudges On, Reincarnation or Not

By the time Brittany was four years old, Sheila and I had decided to divorce. We went our separate ways and agreed on a plan of shared custody of our daughter. Brittany would stay with Sheila for one week, and then me for one week, Sheila for two weeks, and then back to my house for a week. Then the schedule would repeat.

It was a bit confusing, but I did not want to be a weekend dad. I wanted to play a day-to-day role in my daughter's life. Brittany and I have always had a very close relationship. We were more than just father and daughter; we were like best friends.

Apparently believing a man *should* be married, I took my fourth and last stab at matrimonial bliss with Balinda, a woman I met doing community theatre. The union lasted about a year and a half, and the only good thing to come of it was my son, McCartney or "Mac." Mac was six years younger than Brittany. The custody arrangement for him was more typical. Mac lived with his mother in another town but was close enough he could stay at our house every other weekend. Like most kids, Britt and Mac argued fervently one minute and played together like the best of friends the next. But the age difference *made* a difference. By the time she was twelve and he was six, Brittany had become very protective of her little brother.

After my latest matrimonial fiasco, I became the theatre critic for a weekly newspaper, the *Nashville PRIDE*. This allowed me to continue with my writing—and also provided free tickets to plays and movies, giving Brittany, Mac, and me weekend activities.

Before long, I was using my degrees again and teaching theatre and speech at Cumberland University. During the weeks Brittany came to stay with me, my mother lived with us so I could work. My mom took Brittany to school, picked her up, then served as a live-in babysitter till I got home from work. As a result, Brittany and "Mima" (as she dubbed her grandma) became very close— probably much closer than they would have been if Sheila and I had remained married.

I also directed school plays at Cumberland and usually also taught summer classes while directing shows at theatres in Nashville. My free time was spent with my two kids. I guess I finally learned my matrimonial lesson after my divorce with McCartney's mother in 1993. I have never remarried.

Every other weekend, McCartney visited us. I'd drive the sixty miles to Murfreesboro, Tennessee, to pick him up, and he'd join in on whatever activity was going on at my house. Mac and Brittany were very close growing up. But McCartney was always a huge devotee of any kind of sports, and that put him at a disadvantage at my house because I never cared anything at all about team sports. But there was plenty else to do. We all three loved to swim, and I had a membership at the local YMCA. So we spent lots of time in the pool. Board games were a major diversion, with Mac usually ending up the winner—he's extremely intelligent. Lots of movies, lots of plays, and of course, the kids would frequently accompany me to rehearsals for whatever play I happened to be working on at the time.

Ouija Gets a Second (and Ominous) Life

My old circa-1974 Ouija board was still around—and I had told the kids the stories of my adventures chatting with Patience and other entities, so they were familiar with the concept. One evening when Brittany was about nine or ten, she had several little girls over for a sleepover, they unearthed the Ouija, dusted it off, and brought it to me. I had been grading papers, but I put my work aside. Apparently they had been telling each other ghost stories, and Britt had chimed in with a few Patience Worth/Ouija episodes I'd shared with her. One thing led to another, and they wanted to try their hands at some Ouija magic. Since my own experiences with Ouija had always been totally harmless and fun, I didn't see any reason not to show them how it worked.

I briefed them on the basic techniques and they partnered up and gave it a whirl. At first nothing much happened. Their only responses were useless gibberish. Finally, I volunteered to participate. Brittany and I started getting yes and no answers to questions—then simple sentences. This loosened everyone up, and the other little girls started getting results without me. I went back to grading my papers.

So from then until Brittany was fifteen, we'd occasionally take out the Ouija board and have fun with it. I truly considered it all a harmless game. Sometimes we'd pick up Patience, but more often than not, we'd tune in to some lonesome spirit mostly wanting to talk about the woeful events surrounding their own demise. Naturally, Brittany was full of questions concerning whatever boy she was interested in at the time—or she would want to hear predictions concerning her future. It didn't do much good to tell her that if these really were spirits, they probably didn't have any clearer insight into her future than she did. Occasionally, McCartney sat in on these sessions with the spirits—but he was never as interested in it as Britt was. But treks into the paranormal world, via Ouija or me telling ghost stories, played only a very minor part in our lives.

In 1995, I had to have two spinal operations due to a staph infection I'd picked up on a camping trip. I am told that I nearly died, but my immediate concern was that it was the most agonizing pain I'd ever felt. I was in and out of the hospital for a year, so without tenure, I had to give up my teaching position. However, I continued with my theatre critiques, writing and editing at the *Nashville PRIDE*.

Chapter 3
Spiritual Underpinnings

I had joined the Episcopal church in Lebanon around 1978. I had been Roman Catholic, but my wife at the time, Linda, was reared Presbyterian. This Episcopal church was our compromise—all the pomp and ceremony of the Catholics for me, but no uncomfortable trips to confession for her. Later when I married Sheila, she also joined the Episcopal church. After my final divorce, from Balinda, Britt and I joined another Episcopal church in our new community within metro Nashville.

After my staph infection brush with the Grim Reaper, we became very involved in the church, attending regularly. I even took a position on the parish council and became close friends with the priest and his wife. Brittany had been baptized as a baby at the Episcopal church in Lebanon, and I had McCartney baptized at our new church when he was five.

But my interest in the paranormal never subsided. I continued to read books and was particularly taken with the works of the "sleeping prophet" Edgar Cayce, the psychic Ruth Montgomery, and the Bridey Murphy reincarnation story.

By now Nashville had become the home of several paranormal/occult bookstores. One Saturday afternoon, while perusing the latest offerings, I saw a notice tacked by the cash register advertising a class in Wicca that would be offered at the shop. All I knew about Wicca at the time had been gleaned from TV and a recent movie with Sandra Bullock and Nicole Kidman called *Practical Magic*. I asked the young woman at the cash register about the class, and it turned out she was the teacher. She explained the proposed curricula and gave me a brief outline of what she intended to teach. She said the course wasn't designed to convert anyone to Wicca or any Pagan religion, but rather was intended purely for informational purposes. She'd lay the facts out and allow the students to draw their own conclusions. I was fascinated and signed up for the course.

Brittany and I continued to attend the Episcopal church, and I didn't see my newfound interest in Wicca as a conflict. I simply found the idea of this nature-based religion intriguing and wanted to learn as much about it as possible. I read a few books on Wicca, and occasionally Brittany had questions about the course I'd answer. I learned quite a bit and developed a soft spot in my heart for the nature-based Pagan religions.

The course even required me to try a few of the Wiccan rituals honoring the Goddess (and a male god figure more like a mischievous Pan than the Bible's vengeful Yahweh) at the time of the full moon. I genuinely felt a spiritual surge in the process, but I believe that God is God no matter what you call him/her and no matter the method of reverence.

Brittany, now about fourteen, was intrigued by the notion of Wicca—more, I think, because she found it inviting that practitioners cast spells to modify their everyday realities, rather than that she had any real interest in a nature-based explanation of the cosmos. But I believe that any personal exploration into one's spiritual side is a good thing as long as it brings one closer to God in some way.

A Ghost in the Cemetery

In 1999, I learned that my childhood housekeeper/nanny had passed away. Maggie had come to be a part of my family when I was five years old. She was a large, robust, jovial African American woman who was hired to keep house and watch me while my mother worked as the bookkeeper for my father's real estate/construction company. I was an only child, and it seemed that 75 percent of the time Maggie and I *were* the household. She had no formal education past grammar school, but was extremely intelligent, witty, and gregarious.

Maggie worked for my family for eleven years, finally leaving when I was sixteen after my father died and the money dried up. She had been a major influence on my upbringing and played a huge role in shaping me into the man I became. Many years later, her death would have a profound effect on me—probably even more so because I didn't learn of it for several months after she died. Granted, we hadn't remained close after she quit working for us—but my mom and I still went to her house and visited with her on occasion. I even took Brittany, and later McCartney, to meet Maggie—but these visits would have been after Maggie had gotten along in years. They never knew the Maggie I grew up with.

By the time I learned of Maggie's passing, all I could do was go to visit her grave. She was buried in a national military cemetery in Nashville because her last husband had been a soldier in World War II. I stood at her grave remembering how much she had meant to me and shed more than a few tears for the woman who had been as important to me at one time as my own mother. Then I started walking back to the car parked nearby.

When I got back to my '89 Sterling sedan, I was startled to see a little old lady sitting in the backseat. I had quick memory flashes of the ghost I had seen standing at the foot of my bed eight or nine years earlier. I could see her in great detail, but I could also see right through her. This wasn't Maggie. In my car sat an elderly white woman with gray hair wearing one of those pillbox hats that had been popular back in the sixties. She was dressed in her Sunday best. She was very thin, almost tiny, prim and proper, sitting there bolt-upright, and looking at me from inside the glass as if to say, "Well, let's go. I'm ready to leave." Just like the other time I had seen an apparition, there was absolutely nothing scary about it. At that moment, it just seemed perfectly natural. I shook my head as if to tell her I wasn't accepting riders and she'd have to stay in the cemetery—and when I did that, she was gone in a flash.

I told the kids about my brush with this Miss Daisy, and naturally they were fascinated—just as they were with my ghost stories about the Bell Witch and my other personal paranormal run-ins with the unseen. Both kids were always interested in these relatively spooky tales, but the paranormal really did not play any kind of major part in our lives until Brittany was fifteen. Then suddenly one night without warning, the paranormal came back into my life with a vengeance. At the risk of sounding cliché, life would inalterably change for all of us, especially Brittany.

Everything in the Prison

During the spring of 1999, I directed a play called *Everything in the Garden* for a local community theatre company. The theatre group rehearsed and produced their shows in a facility called the Nashville Music Institute, which had an auditorium and numerous rehearsal rooms where classes in various musical instruments were taught during the day. The building itself was quite old and was one of the oldest brick structures in Nashville—dating back to the early 1800s. The building was originally built to be the Tennessee State Prison.

Brittany frequently went to rehearsals with me and helped out later with the actual production, assisting with makeup and backstage work during performances. The cast and crew of any theatrical production often becomes very close, almost like family, during rehearsals and the actual production. No one is getting paid, but everyone is having fun. Brittany fit right in and was very popular with everyone involved in the show. She was fourteen and attending a public high school devoted to the visual and performing arts. One of the cast members was a teenaged girl about Brittany's age and they became quick friends.

As with any building that old, the Nashville Music Institute came complete with its own ghost stories. The daytime music staff talked of doors opening and closing by themselves, unexplained noises, and sightings of supposed apparitions of prisoners and their guards. I took all that with a grain of salt, noticing that the music teachers telling these tales seemed to be seriously enjoying the wide-eyed responses they'd get from our actors—particularly those two teenaged girls.

The institute was a three-story building, seemingly rambling off in all directions, especially if you're alone in the dark trying to find a light switch. It wasn't unusual for actors to wander off and get lost. One evening during a dress rehearsal, the actors were sitting in the communal dressing room putting on their makeup. Somebody brought up the topic of the ghosts the music teachers had told us about. I was only half listening, because I was just passing through on my way to make sure all the props were set on the backstage prop table. I made my way to the backstage area and busied myself with the millions of things a director has to do before the curtain can go up.

Maybe fifteen minutes later, one of the stagehands rushed up to tell me that something was wrong with Brittany. She was hysterical because of something she'd seen upstairs. However by the time I got to her, the reported hysteria had subsided. But she did run up to me and hug me like she was afraid I'd disappear if she didn't.

I tried to calm Brittany down and make as little of the incident as possible in order to keep everyone else calm—with curtain in less than half an hour we didn't need any added stress.

Trembling, Brittany told me she had gone upstairs alone to the top floor and wandered around in the empty rooms. Entering one near the back of the building, she'd seen a man seated in a chair wearing a judge's gown holding a knife. In his lap rested a severed, bloody head. He looked at her and then pointed his knife at her, motioning for her to come closer. Obviously that was all the freak show she needed, so she turned on her heels and rushed back through the rooms and downstairs.

She begged me to go up for myself and investigate. So I turned the production over to my assistant and headed upstairs to see for myself. But I found nothing other than classrooms and confusing halls. The electricity was on and all the switches worked, so I made my way back to the room where Britt had supposedly seen the apparition. I was a bit apprehensive, but frankly more concerned with my production than seeing specters.

Having seen a couple of ghosts myself, I didn't doubt her. By this time, I was convinced that she could see spirits. Aside from the lady she kept seeing as a toddler in our old Victorian house, she had occasionally reported other non-threatening sightings. The two ghosts I had seen also seemed quite benign. But Brittany's latest sighting didn't sound like Casper the friendly ghost. He seemed to be a ghoulish judge with a knife and was cradling a victim's head in his lap.

As I rumbled through the classrooms, I was thinking that if Brittany really had seen an apparition, it was probably just toying with her mind—projecting itself as whatever it thought would scare her. So no judge with a bloody knife was lurking about waiting to pounce on me. Since I didn't find anything out of the ordinary, I went back downstairs. By the time I got to the makeup room, Brittany was helping an actor put her makeup on and chattering about the upcoming show. I took her aside and told her that I hadn't found anything but was careful to say that I did not doubt that she had. I gently reprimanded her for going into an area we'd been told not to and told her not to wander off in the building alone again. She was more interested in getting back to work with makeup than talking to me about spooks—so we all returned our concentration to the show.

After the curtain went down that evening and the cast and crew went out to a restaurant, the conversation inevitably returned to Brittany's encounter with the judge. In fact, this particular cast's interests often turned to the paranormal (no doubt because of all the ghost stories surrounding where we were producing our play). Of course, I always responded with stories about Patience Worth and the Ouija board whenever the topic went otherworldly.

Directing *Everything in the Garden* at the Nashville Music Institute came at the same time I was taking that course in Wicca— so I was overtly interested with anything and everything in the spiritual realm. The incidents in the old prison building had also caused Brittany, most everyone in my cast and crew, and myself to want some answers to our paranormal questions.

Legends of ghosts in the music institute were on everyone's mind with my cast and crew. If we weren't talking about the play itself, the conversation inevitably drifted to the haunted building we were in—and the paranormal in general.

A young married couple working in the play mentioned they felt their home was having paranormal activity and asked if I knew of a psychic who could help. I recommended my friend Laurel, and she agreed to do a house cleansing.

So the next Sunday afternoon, Laurel, Brittany, and I met the couple at their modern-style, board and batten home outside of Nashville.

This would be the first time Brittany would work with Laurel to remove spirits from places where they shouldn't be. By this time I knew that Brittany had abilities to perceive those in astral dimensions, and I was delighted and appreciative to have someone like Laurel help her understand and sculpt her talents.

Laurel's mother had been a sensitive too and helped ease her into experiencing the metaphysical world. She said it could be "a freaky world if you didn't understand what all these new sensations were." So I was delighted that Laurel was willing to be there for Britt during what could be a confusing time.

The house cleansing, however, proved to be relatively uneventful. But Britt at least had a chance to see Laurel in action.

Chapter 4
The Séance

The artistic director of the theatre company I was directing for was a jolly, rotund gent by the name of Joel Meriwether, who was also deeply interested in the supernatural. Joel had just recently opened himself up to channeling spirits, or going into a trance-like state and allowing the spirit of some deceased entity to speak through him. Of course, this can be an extremely risky and dangerous practice—but none of us really realized it at the time.

One night after the show, a group of actors, Joel, Brittany, and I decided to go back to my condo and get out my old Ouija board—maybe have a séance to see if we could get the spirits to tell us what was going on in the music institute. I always hoped that Patience might show up and help out, but sometimes that happened and sometimes it didn't. I had learned in my Wicca course about casting a protective circle with sea salt around the area to be used for any ritual and to ask for guidance and protection from the God and Goddess before doing anything. So armed with salt, candles, and Wicca 101, I felt confident we were going to get some answers.

Balancing a few invisible spirits just didn't appear to me to be that big a deal. So I cast a protective circle around my kitchen table, and six of us sat down to have our séance. For whatever reason, Patience was missing in action.

We asked to speak to a spirit who could tell us what was going on in the music institute. Mostly all we got were bits and pieces of useless disjointed phrases and threats from several entities claiming to be demons or even Satan himself. Frankly, to me this just seemed humorous. But nothing physical happened. No flickering candles, no rampaging furniture, no voices from beyond. Just some seemingly lame threats, and no information about the music institute other than a warning of not to go back there or we'd all be sorry.

Since we felt the Ouija board had failed to give us any useful information, Joel volunteered to try and channel a helpful spirit. We figured we didn't have anything to lose, so why not? He took deep breaths and after a minute seemed to pass out. His head slumped onto his chest. I had seen him channel before at a cast party, so I wasn't afraid he was incapacitated or anything. Sure enough, after a couple of seconds, he looked up as if he'd never seen any of us before and smiled a huge Cheshire cat grin. I believe he said he was a spirit from the ancient civilization of Atlantis. But there was no useful information, other than a prediction that Brittany would marry a hockey player. After nearly three decades, numerous boyfriends and an ex-husband, I have yet to see a hockey player.

Joel came out of his trance none the worse for ware, and things started to wind down. So with nothing much to show for it, our séance came to an end. The teenagers were getting sleepy, and several of the adults had had a bit too much to drink. It was getting late, and we all had to get up and do a Sunday afternoon matinee. But although the séance had been apparently non-productive, I would come to believe in less than a year that perhaps we had stirred something up with the Ouija board that night in my kitchen. We had received seemingly harmless, even bogus threats from entities claiming to be demons. Frankly at the time, I thought it was funny and said so. But our contact with this negative energy may have led to more serious incidents about to slap my family in the face. I guess I'll never know if there was a connection, but from that evening forward, my family noticed a discernable, slightly ominous gloom in my innocuous little condo.

The First "Love of Her Life"

Brittany would have a string of boyfriends—the first being a guy named Chase she met at school that fall. Chase was a very intelligent, talented musician, almost painfully quiet and shy. I can't really attest to his character, because he'd usually clam up around me. But Brittany was positively smitten with him. He was her first boyfriend, and she was convinced that she was madly in love.

One of their favorite activities was trying to contact spirits on the Ouija board. Neither of them had a car, so all their dates were either at my house, his parent's house in another suburb fifteen miles away, or at Sheila's house. Sheila did not own a Ouija board, but at my house Britt had apparently retrieved the Ouija board from underneath my bed and taken it to her room—but honestly, at the time I wouldn't have cared.

My own contacts with Chase were limited, but I remember one Saturday afternoon when I was painting the inside of the condo. Chase's mother brought him over to help us paint. I believe

I saw him take a few swipes at the living room wall with the brush I gave him, but it wasn't long before he and Brittany disappeared upstairs to her room. I could hear them talking up there, giving me evidence that he actually could speak.

"I played Ouija with Chase almost every time he came over," she eventually explained. "We talked to things over and over again claiming to be the devil, claiming to be a demon. I guess I opened a door to let them in with that thing. I was obsessive over it. I wanted to do it all the time, even if it scared me. I was enthralled with it."

Whenever Brittany and Chase asked to communicate with a spirit, they would usually get an entity answering teenage questions about love, school, and friends—often claiming to be able to predict the future. What high school kid could resist the allure of such an omniscient entity with apparent keys to their future? Nevertheless, there were telltale negative signs left by the entity/entities that even a couple of fifteen-year-olds should have picked up on.

Brittany says the "nice spirit" would always, eventually, turn the floor over to something of a much nastier nature. This one would claim to be a demon or even Satan himself when pressed for an identity. When asked what exactly it wanted from them, it would answer: "your soul" and assert that it wanted to see them "burn."

There is infinite good in the universe, but there is also lurking evil. The kids didn't know that, and I didn't even know they were playing with the Ouija board. But by making their consciousnesses available to other dimensions via the Ouija board, they may have literally opened themselves up subconsciously to something very bad indeed.

Safe, Happy Ouija Makes for a Safe, Happy User

I know now that tampering with metaphysical implements like the Ouija board is not a harmless pursuit. It can be extremely dangerous, perhaps even life threatening. But in 1999, I was convinced that involvement in spirit communications was all about managing who you spoke to. The few times I had encountered negative (or even self-proclaimed evil) entities, there were no significant repercussions—mostly just blustering threats. Ouija was just a fascinating game and a great topic of conversation.

I was wrong and very naive in my attitude about the Ouija board. Spirit communication can be harmless and fun, and it can be beneficial. But it can also lead to very, very negative and even evil things. But all this I had to learn the hard way.

Use of the Ouija board opens up a portal or gateway to the astral dimensions for spirits to come in. Communicating with spirits via the Ouija board can be a useful tool *if* the proper precautions are taken. Since my primary objective for writing this book is to help other families avoid the trauma my family went through as a result of Ouija board *misuse*, here are some easy precautions I've learned. This should ensure that you reap the benefits of spirit communication while avoiding the potentially dangerous pitfalls.

Before using the board, draw a circle around it with sea salt. Other protective methods include placing quartz crystals around the board to cleanse and maintain energy. Also, hematite or obsidian stones placed at each corner can be used for protection. Some authorities recommend burning lavender incense to attract good spirits. Frankincense, myrrh, or dragon's blood incense are also thought to protect against evil spirits, as is burning sage.

A protective prayer may be the best thing you can do to protect the individuals involved and the environment itself, for example: "I clear this space of all negative energy, and of all the negative energy of spirits who do not belong in this household. I ask that the clearing be positive, and that all of the energy be returned to its source." Cleansing the board after use with incense or sage is also recommended.

Eileen and I never took any of these precautions in New Orleans. Neither did I for the following twenty-five years. But we were lucky—or perhaps Patience was always there to protect us from the "ithers." But when my daughter started experimenting with the Ouija board as a teenager, no precautions were taken—and I suppose Patience wasn't always there to protect her.

Brittany Plays Betsy Bell

In the fall of 2000, Brittany was cast to play the part of Betsy Bell in a stage production of my friend Joel's original play *The Bell Witch of Robertson County*, which he was also directing at the Nashville Music Institute (yep, that same theatre building where Britt had encountered the apparition of the spirit of a judge, or at least something pretending to look like one). Joel had long been fascinated with the legend of the Bell Witch, just as I had. He'd written quite a nice dramatization of the nineteenth-century haunting of the John Bell family. In Joel's version, Betsy had been sexually abused by her father, John, and this abuse could have had something to do with triggering the supernatural phenomenon that became infamous throughout the U.S. and Europe.

Joel is a masterful showman, so I expected this to be a first-rate community theatre performance. Britt was extremely excited about being cast in such a large role. In Joel's *Bell Witch*, Betsy Bell is essentially the lead, and Brittany really put her heart and soul into the part of Betsy Bell.

During their rehearsal period, Britt and I went up to the old Bell Witch farm in Adams, Tennessee, and took the tour they offer tourists. The early 1820s home where the haunting took place has long since been torn down. But there is a museum with a tour available of the wooded property upon which the Bell farm was headquartered. The tour meanders through the thick forest where Betsy and her brothers and sisters played and where many of the incidents in the 1890s M.V. Ingram book about the haunting took place.

These are the woods where the Bell family supposedly saw the spirit of a little girl dressed in green velvet hanging from the branches of various trees. Of course, if anyone attempted to communicate with her, she'd vanish. There were also numerous sightings of a very large black dog with red eyes, snarling and threatening Bell family members and chasing slaves who'd venture too far from their cabins late at night. On the numerous occasions when John Bell would fire his musket at the dog, it would disappear into the mist. When Britt and I were there, the guided trek ended up with a tour of the Bell Witch Cave, where several incidents in the legend took place and where folks in Adams say the spirit resides to this day.

The middle-aged couple running the museum and tour live on the property in a brick home built over a hundred years after the haunting. They claim that not a night goes by they don't hear footsteps in the hallway outside their bedroom, accompanied by unexplained noises—the most dramatic of which is the oft repeated sound in the dining room of dishes being hurled from their china cabinet and dashed to the floor. The crash is so loud, you'd think they would find the hardwood floor covered with shards of broken chinaware and glass. But upon inspecting the carnage, nothing is ever amiss. After having their sleep interrupted by nightly dashes out of bed to inspect the supposed damage, they finally just learned to live with these paranormal audio effects. Now they just roll over and go back to sleep.

The tour guide will point out spots where events in the haunting were said to have taken place and generally creates an ambiance of foreboding and dread—without going overboard, because there are usually children along for the wooded romp. The day Britt and I took the tour, we were the only customers, so the guide poured the possibilities of impending supernatural presences on pretty thick. But during a lull in the guide's narrative as we rounded a bend in the leaf covered pathway, Brittany jerked her head to the side exclaiming, "Ow!" She looked genuinely startled and more than a little annoyed. I asked her what was wrong, and she said she felt like her hair had been pulled. The tour guide rather nonchalantly said, "That happens sometimes with women on the tour. They sometimes feel like someone pulled their hair." I knew from reading numerous accounts of the Bell Witch that one of the spirit's favorite tricks to play on poor Betsy was pulling her hair.

At the time, I took that as another sign of the psychic awareness Laurel had been telling me for years Brittany possessed. Objectively, it could also have been an overly active imagination fueled by her knowledge of the legend or even the tour guide's shtick. But her reaction to the feeling of having her hair pulled was immediate and spontaneous. The moment wasn't anything we dwelled upon, and before long we were again immersed in the tour guide's banter.

During the production of *The Bell Witch of Robertson County*, Britt didn't report any paranormal sightings of apparitions at the music institute or any other worldly events going on during rehearsals. The show was successful, got great reviews, and Britt gave a tremendous performance—and I was especially proud of her for wanting to go to Adams and see where the real Betsy Bell lived as preparation for her role.

Chapter 5

Prelude to the Nightmare

One morning at about ten a.m. during the Christmas holidays with the kids out of school, McCartney, my mother, and I were downstairs. Mom was reading the newspaper, I was checking my email and having coffee, and McCartney was playing with his action figures on the floor. Brittany was still upstairs asleep. Twenty minutes later, we all heard knocking and banging on the walls upstairs. At first I thought it might be someone in the adjacent condo hanging a picture. But it sounded much louder than a picture-hanging venture should have, so I went upstairs to investigate. The knocking continued and got even louder. I looked in on Brittany, who was oblivious to the noise and still sound asleep. The loud banging continued as I watched her lying there sleeping. I could tell then that the banging seemed to be coming from the other side of her wall, so I figured maybe the guy next door was doing some work in his bathroom. However, after looking outside, I realized the guy next door wasn't home. No car in his parking space. As a salesman, he was frequently gone for long periods anyway, so that wasn't unusual.

The banging on the walls stopped, so I went back downstairs. After maybe five minutes, it started up again—much louder this time. It still seemed to be coming from the other side of Brittany's wall. I looked in on her again, and she was still fast asleep. My mother thought there were workmen outside, maybe on the roof, so she went outside to check that out. Mima came back in and announced there were no workmen anywhere to be seen.

Now the banging started up a third time. Loud was now getting louder still. I went upstairs again to find that Britt was still asleep. I woke her up this time and asked her if she'd heard anything. The moment I woke her, the banging stopped. She said she hadn't heard anything, but she'd been dreaming that "people were knocking on the wall." So I went back downstairs, and Britt got up to get dressed.

Maybe five minutes later, the pounding started again—ending in a loud crashing thud. Britt called out in a weak little voice for me to come upstairs. She was standing in the hallway, looking into my bedroom with one of those "Oh, my God!" expressions on her face. The heavy, wooden bench that sits in front of my dresser had overturned. It was now next to the foot of my bed on its side. Sheets and pillows that had been piled on top of the bench in anticipation of making up my bed were crumpled on the floor leaning against it.

Brittany said she had glanced into my room on her way to the bathroom when the banging had started up that last time. She claimed the bench levitated a couple of feet above the carpeted floor, then slung itself toward the opposite wall maybe eight feet away and hurled itself to the floor. That would have been the loud thud we'd heard downstairs as a climax to the last series of pounding. Brittany was quite agitated, but I coaxed her into coming downstairs, where we all sat around the table as she explained what she had just seen for McCartney and Mima. I calmed her down, and she went back upstairs to take her shower.

I do believe such unexplained phenomena *can* happen, and Brittany had no reason to make this up. She was more than just a little shaken. But I had to run a few errands, and McCartney went with me. Mima was left in charge. We were gone no more than forty-five minutes.

When we got back, she met us at the door, sobbing hysterically. She had been unaware that Mac and I were leaving, and she was more than a bit upset that we had left her there even though her grandmother was still home. She said that "no more than three minutes" after she'd gotten into the shower, the pounding on the wall resumed. This time she said it sounded like someone was on the other side of the shower wall, ramming it with something heavy. She said the shower shook and then several bottles of shampoo, conditioner, and other stuff flew off the shelf inside the shower and plummeted to the fiberglass bathtub floor. One thick glass broke, shattering into several pieces as if it had been hurled with significant force—not as if it had just fallen off the shelf. Luckily, she was unharmed.

During the next couple of months, the pounding on the walls continued intermittently at inopportune times—often at night when I was at home by myself, and sometimes on the nights Brittany was staying with me. At the time, I was putting the finishing touches on my play about Shakespeare and Edward de Vere, the Earl of Oxford, *A Rose by Any Other Name,* to be produced by the Athens South Theatre Co. in Nashville's historic Belcourt Theatre. I did most of my work writing late at night on the computer at my desk just beneath and to the side of the stairway.

As I'd sit at my desk working at two a.m., I'd often hear what sounded like someone humming on the stairway just above where I was sitting. It got to be a common occurrence for me to experience what sounded like a woman or a child humming just above me around one or two o'clock in the morning. All I have to do is look up, and I can see almost to the top of the stairs—and naturally, there would never be anyone there. You would think this would be an unsettling moment, but actually it wasn't. I never felt threatened or afraid—but the humming could definitely interrupt your train of thought. Usually, I would rationalize the music someone was making by attributing it to the neighbors—even though I knew that the condo to the left of mine was empty at the time, and the one on the right housed a family with school children who went to bed early.

But life went on. As I finished my play and conducted the business of preparing for the production, Christmastime approached and the kids were let out of school for the holidays.

Chapter 6
The Holy Water Incident

I was supposed to have dinner with two theatre associates of mine, Evans and Ann Donnell, on Monday evening, January 8, 2001, to discuss plans for the upcoming production of my play. That morning I had told Brittany I needed to go to this working dinner, and she didn't seem to care. However, as time neared for me to leave, she became noticeably agitated.

School was only in session half a day that day, so I picked Britt and her friend Jennifer up at about eleven a.m. Jennifer had decided to come to our house, where the girls planned to watch movies. While they watched their movies on VHS, I worked on that week's theatre review for the newspaper. Afterward, I went upstairs and took a shower to prepare to go to Evans's house, where I needed to be at seven p.m. After I showered, I told the girls that Jennifer would need to call her mom to come pick her up, or she could leave with me and I'd drop her off.

Then out of the blue, Brittany started begging me not to go. She was jittery and seemed frightened of something. This was very much unlike her. I often rehearsed at night and Britt stayed home with her grandmother who lived with me part-time to help out. Usually she was more than happy to see me go. Now back in those days we still had dial-up and you couldn't connect with the internet while someone else was on the phone. My absence would give her time to play on the internet without being pestered by me to get off the computer so I could make calls.

I really didn't know how long my meeting was going to last, and school would be back in session the next day. This was a school night, and Britt wasn't really allowed to stay at a friend's house on school nights.

But Britt actually started crying, begging me not to go. I knew she was still upset about the banging and pounding on the walls we'd been experiencing for the last few weeks. She had also been more than a little apprehensive about going upstairs by herself, particularly to take a shower. So I asked my mother to accompany Britt upstairs when she took her shower and maybe sit in the bathroom with her so that she wouldn't be afraid—and I told Brittany this. This plan seemed to help, but she was still tearful and didn't want me to go.

But I had to, so I dropped Jennifer off at her apartment and proceeded to Evans's house about twenty miles away on the other side of town. I was very worried about Britt, so when I got to Evans's I called home to see if she was okay. The line was busy, so I figured she was on the internet. We went ahead and had dinner.

Since I knew both Ann and Evans were open to metaphysical ideas, I told them about the wall-pounding incident. Ann then said she thought she had just what I needed. She went into another part of their house and came back with a small bottle of holy water she had obtained at her Greek Orthodox church. She explained that she usually gets a bottle every year during the Epiphany season, but for some reason had felt she needed to pick up two this year. She said, "I believe this one was meant for you to have."

Ann went on to explain how I should sprinkle holy water around the house to "protect it from evil influences." Also, since Brittany seemed to be the object of all the odd activity, it would be a good idea to sprinkle some of it on her forehead as personal protection for her. I'd never done anything like this before, but it seemed like an appropriate plan to me.

After dinner and our discussion about the production, I tried calling Britt again, but the line was still busy. So I took my bottle of holy water and returned home. I was unusually anxious and found myself driving over the speed limit to get there faster. As I drove, I prayed to God, the Goddess, and any other powerful supernatural beings that might be willing to help protect Brittany from whatever it was she was so afraid of that evening.

When I arrived home, Brittany came out to the car to meet me. She volunteered that she hadn't taken that bath, because an email friend had called her from Louisiana and talked for three hours. He was the boyfriend of a friend of Britt's, so I think they'd mostly talked about Britt's friend.

I showed her the little bottle of holy water and explained to her what it was for—and how we needed to sprinkle it around the house and on her to protect from evil forces. At first she seemed to be very supportive of this idea and wanted to help me.

Britt followed me upstairs, and we began the ritual in my room. I removed the lid and started sprinkling the holy water all about the room. But after a few minutes, she seemed to lose much of her initial interest. While I sprinkled, she sat on the side of my bed and just watched. I didn't take much notice of her behavior and mostly attributed it to typical teenager moodiness.

After I felt the room was sufficiently sprinkled, I told Brittany what Ann had said about the need to sprinkle a bit of it on her to protect her too.

At this, she became even more surly, curled up into a ball on the bed, and covered her face. She simply said, "No, I don't want that." I suddenly had a sinking feeling in the pit of my stomach. I feared that I knew the reason for her reluctance, but I just couldn't believe it was happening. Hoping that I was just being silly, I kind of laughed a little and told her that this was just something that had to be done.

As she lay on the bed, I sprinkled a bit of the holy water on her forehead—but she tried to shield her face. As the water touched her skin, she recoiled as if I'd poured battery acid on her.

Each time I sprinkled a bit more holy water on her, she grimaced in pain and cried out. She started to get up and move away from me. Without a real clue as to what to do, I just instinctively held her down and doused more water on her hair. After a few moments, my daughter relaxed, shuddered, and said, "They don't like that." Thinking whatever was in her had been forced to vacate and the worst of it was over, I began leading her out into the hallway. I told Britt we needed to sprinkle her room too.

As we entered Brittany's room, she began pulling against me and saying that she didn't want to "go in there." All this was starting to really scare me, but I felt there was no going back. Once we got inside Britt's room, she became belligerent—aggressively fighting to get away from me. The distorted expression on her face was one I'll never forget.

She strangely, somehow, no longer looked like my daughter. Although the facial characteristics were the same, I've never seen anyone look out at me through eyes that expressed such hate and malevolence.

"I'll kill her; you can't stop me," the force within her spat out.

Totally petrified but knowing I had to finish what I'd started, I tightened my grip on her. Whatever this was, it projected more maleficence than anything I'd ever encountered. Although I was looking at my daughter, a being I loved more than anything in the world, I felt I was in the presence of something absolutely despicable.

I tossed another liberal dose of holy water on her forehead, and she flung herself onto the floor. Snarling as she crawled toward the wall, she clawed her fingernails deep into the carpet. Down on all fours, she sounded more like a wild beast than a fifteen-year-old girl. Once she reached the corner of the room, she repeatedly banged her head against the wall in what appeared to be an attempt to knock herself unconscious. She was still down on her elbows and knees.

Afraid she was going to seriously hurt herself, I knelt beside Brittany and grabbed her arms, pulling her away from the wall. I was on my knees, holding her down. She was flailing at the air, trying to hit me and kicking at me with her feet. Loudly cursing me, she screamed out that God was dead and that I also would be soon. She was lightly foaming at the mouth and spitting in my direction, though I was able to dodge the spittle. Her eyes rolled back into her head so that only the whites were visible. She thrust her tongue out at some distance, exploring the world with it as if she were a serpent. I truly did not know that a tongue could extend that far. Then her eyes reappeared. Although her expression was as purely evil as anything I'd ever seen, the eyes had a look of wonderment in them as if they'd never looked out at the world before. The effect was similar to how a tiny baby looks at the world, but a vengeful baby.

She began kicking me, and I had to sit on her legs to avoid the kicks. Meanwhile, I held her wrists to avoid being scratched or hit. She had suddenly grown extremely strong, exerting more power in her movements than I would have thought her capable. I continued to sprinkle the holy water, and this seemed to be the only real weapon I had. It was becoming more and more difficult to keep her down.

Although I was terrified, I also found myself becoming furious with this thing that was trying to steal my daughter. I continued dousing her with holy water, determined I would not let it have my little girl!

About this time, the entity told me, "We've been in here for a year."

Not knowing what else to do, I started calling Brittany's name.

"We have her now, and we'll never let her come out," it snarled.

"No, you don't have anything. You're just air; you're nothing more than a deranged idea. Let me speak to my daughter!" I tossed another dash of holy water.

Suddenly Britt's demeanor changed. Instead of the grotesque mask of hate I had just been looking at, my little girl came back. Her eyes were filled with tears. It was the most heart-wrenching thing I've ever seen.

"Daddy, help me," she uttered in a tiny voice.

"Don't worry, sweetie, Daddy's here. Everything's going to be okay." I kissed her on the forehead and held her tight. I told her I wouldn't let anything harm her and to hang in there.

"I can't hold on. They're too strong. They won't let me go. Bye, Daddy, I love you."

I felt desperation, despair, and the widest array of negative, poor self-image emotions conceivable. I began talking to Brittany about fun things that we had done in the past.

"Remember that camping trip we took to Fall Creek Falls State Park?" I asked her, trying to make her change her focus. I described several things we'd done on the trip. She looked up at me and smiled weakly.

"You know the first time I ever saw you smile?" I asked, shaking with fear that this terrible gargoyle might return at any moment. "You were just a little baby sitting in a car seat on the kitchen counter. I was getting ready to take you out and put you in the car. You looked up at me and smiled." I related that story and a couple more. These memories from her past as the true Brittany seemed to help her hold on.

"Daddy, I didn't even know they were in there," she weakly volunteered.

"It's okay, sweetie."

Then, with a powerful surge, it kicked and bucked and nearly threw me off. My nearly eighty-year-old mother, who was staying with us for the week, was downstairs. She heard the commotion and rushed upstairs as quickly as she could.

Nearly hysterical herself, she asked what on earth was going on. Not having the time to explain, I just motioned for her to help me. She told me later that she thought Brittany was having some kind of seizure. My mom knelt down and aided in holding Brittany, while I continued to dash holy water on her. Britt went limp again as she lay on her stomach on the carpet. I began singing songs that I'd sung to her as a baby and again called her name. She looked up at me and smiled, rolling back over. My mom began massaging her legs as I continued to sing silly, kiddy songs from her childhood. In a wee little voice, Britt started singing too.

Then just as suddenly as it had left, the demon/spirit returned. With an indescribable round of obscenities, the entity spat at Britt's grandmother and again started bucking. By now it was slobbering all over itself. I still held her wrists, but she was flailing with more force than ever. I honestly didn't know how much longer I could hold out.

I told my mother to go downstairs and call Brittany's mother, Sheila. As she left, the entity told me it was taking Brittany to hell and it would see me there soon.

I splashed another volley of holy water on her forehead. Then I looked at the bottle out of the corner of my eye. This was the first time I'd noticed the bottle was becoming empty. I never let on to the demons that I was concerned, but from that point forward I became more conservative with my applications.

Despite their aversion to the holy water, the demons seemed to be getting physically stronger—so I was greatly relieved when my mom returned from calling Sheila to help me hold Britt down. During the fifteen minutes it took Sheila to drive over from her house, Brittany alternated between herself and being possessed by unspeakable evil forces. I could tell that Mima was considerably freaked out by other voices emanating from her granddaughter, but much to her credit, she pitched right in to help and didn't let the weirdness of the situation interfere with assisting me.

My mom was always extremely uncomfortable about any mention of things paranormal because of her own unwanted abilities, but with real evil threatening her granddaughter, she was a trouper. Whenever the true Brittany would emerge, Mima and I would talk to her about things we knew she loved—her friends, trips we'd taken, plays she'd been in—anything that would anchor her in the reality of *our* dimension and not that of the demons'. We both sang songs to her—me, old Beatles tunes I'd sung to her as a baby, and Mima, old pre-World War II songs she'd sung Brittany when she'd babysit her. Sometimes Britt would weakly try to sing the songs too. But when the demons would reappear, she once more cursed and spat, drooled on herself, clawed at us, and kicked wildly.

When Sheila arrived, it took her a moment to actually believe what she was seeing. At first she called out to Brittany as if she could be reasoned with. But after getting no response from her daughter, it only took her a fraction of a moment to cross the room and help out in the restraining process. I quickly filled her in on the events of the last hour.

Sheila, at this point in her life, adhered to a pretty fundamentalist Christian theological view of the universe. She'd been attending a nondenominational local church (which Britt also attended whenever she stayed at her mom's). As I held Brittany to the floor, Sheila leaned over and made the sign of the cross on Britt's forehead with her finger. Even though this whole episode had been prompted by a Christian gesture of repelling evil with holy water, it hadn't occurred to me to try this—and also, possibly because I was just so rattled by everything that was going on, I wasn't think-ing straight. However, Sheila's symbolic act seemed to cause the entity inside Brittany excruciating pain—much the same reaction I'd gotten from the holy water.

Then Sheila began intoning, "In the name of the Father, the Son, and the Holy Spirit, come out." At that, the entity wailed and moaned and was visibly undergoing a great deal of discomfort. Nevertheless, the entity was still vigorously fighting us—trying to free itself by bucking the body it was possessing. As we held Brittany's arms, she dug her nails into our hands. Again, she be-gan spitting at us, lolling her tongue around in all directions like a serpent, and rolling her eyeballs into the backs of their sockets so only the whites of her eyes could be seen. Brittany, controlled by the demon, was working herself up into a complete frenzy, and it was becoming more and more difficult to restrain her.

Seeing the positive effect Sheila's Christian invocations were having, I also called upon the Trinity as I continued to dispense the holy water. During the rare moments when the entity permitted the real Brittany to surface, I would kiss her on the forehead and talk to her about fun activities we'd shared over the years. I'd sing more ridiculous children's songs to her that had been important to her as a youngster. When Sheila saw that this technique was effec-tive in keeping Britt with us longer, she'd join in and sing too. One odd song, in particular, had a soothing effect.

When she was a baby, if Britt was truly upset, nothing much seemed to work—until one day, after exhausting my repertoire of songs, I started singing "Dixie." For some odd reason, she'd always calm down whenever we'd sing the anthem of the Old South to her. No other song worked. So on this most cursed night I sang

"Dixie," and her mother joined in. Like a magic spell, it gave us a much-needed reprieve. At moments when the demon would relinquish its hold on Britt, she would come back to us and weakly join in on singing her favorite babyhood song. It was heartbreaking to hear her sing in that tiny, faraway voice and watch the pain on her tear-drenched face.

But the good moments were few and far between. The demon seemed to be determined to win this battle, and I was becoming particularly concerned because the bottle of holy water was nearly empty. I noticed the entity inside Britt kept looking at the bottle, and I think that it, too, was gauging the amount left.

With all the horror we could handle going on, it was easy to lose track of time. But at some point, Sheila told my mother to call 911. So Mima went into the next room to make the call. As bad as the situation was, I had resisted calling for outside intervention. I kept hoping we could handle this ourselves. I was certain that paramedics and doctors would just think Brittany was crazy. Possessions aren't in most people's daily experience, and I guess maybe I was afraid they would take Britt away from me if they thought she was insane. But I knew what I had been witnessing, so I was certain she was totally and solidly sane. I was and am now convinced the disturbance was being caused by some evil, supernatural being inhabiting her body.

But because of everything we had been through at that point, I didn't know what else to do either. It was becoming obvious that we weren't going to be able to scare the demon away; and now without the holy water, I wasn't sure we could handle it at all.

Britt was still thrashing around, kicking, screaming, and cursing so loudly that when the paramedics finally arrived, I didn't even notice them. But suddenly I realized the room was full of people asking questions. There were three paramedics and three police officers. I was too busy holding Britt down to pay much attention to their uniforms, but I think they were Wilson County Sheriff's deputies. They questioned us about what had been happening, and after we'd filled them in—I was certain they'd think Britt and I both were crazy.

But they didn't try to reach obvious conclusions or judge. They simply did their jobs like true professionals. They suggested we take Britt to the local hospital for observation and to be checked out. She screamed and wailed, protesting that she didn't want to go. At that point I couldn't tell if that was the entity talking or Brittany. But it was obvious that we were going to need help in handling her. I was less than enthused about taking Britt to a hospital, but I was relieved with this short-term solution. It would, at least, give us a chance to catch our breath and regroup. Then, one of the paramedics knelt beside her, took her hand, and was somehow able to calm her down.

During this lull in the chaos, Sheila found a wooden cross on Brittany's dresser that she had made the past summer at an Episcopal summer camp for kids. Britt had made several—one each for Sheila and me, one for her grandmother, and one for herself. Sheila bent over and put the cross around Britt's neck, saying: "Wear this and you'll be all right."

Britt looked up, exhausted and bleary-eyed, and just said, "Okay."

The paramedics went downstairs to get a gurney, and Sheila followed them out, asking how this transport was supposed to work. For a brief moment, I was holding Brittany down by myself. She seemed to be much calmer now, and I thought she had regained some control. I had given her a silver ring with a pentagram on it for Christmas, something she'd asked for. It also included a matching bracelet with little silver pentagrams dangling from it. She had these on at the time. Suddenly she sat up and started trying to take them off and asked me to help her. We got them off and left them on the floor. At the time, I thought maybe that due to the incidents of that night, she had concluded these symbols had some negative (even evil) connotation and wanted to be rid of them. I didn't discover till later that it was the demon that found the pentagram offensive.

The paramedics decided they couldn't get her down the stairs on the stretcher, so I took her by one arm and a paramedic took the other. We walked her slowly down the stairs. Britt was very weak and basically spaced-out, so getting her downstairs wasn't exactly easy.

At the foot of the stairs, the paramedics put Britt onto a stretcher and took her outside. It was cold, and snow was lightly falling. It seemed a night more fit for a peaceful Christmas tableau than the hell we were going through. I could see the ambulance and a couple of police cars, all with their blinking lights piercing the cold night air and ricocheting off each other and the condo townhomes. Without fanfare, Britt was carried out to the ambulance. Instinctively, I felt as though she were being taken away to serve some unjust sentence to hell.

Sheila said she'd drive over behind the ambulance. I grabbed a coat and asked if I could ride with Britt. I was told I couldn't ride in the back with her, but I could sit up front with the driver. I barely noticed our next-door neighbor coming over and talking with my mother. I learned later Mima told him Brittany had had a bad reaction to her medicine. This pacified him, as he said that his mother had also had a seizure once due to a negative reaction to medication. Funny how we are so quick to fabricate stories that rationalize our experiences to fit into others' conceptions of reality.

The trip to the hospital was totally surreal. With the siren screaming like a banshee, the flashing lights framed the ambulance in a kaleidoscope of ungodly illumination. I felt like I was a character in someone else's dream. Through a window in the cab, I could see that Brittany was bucking like a wild horse in the stretcher, but luckily they had her strapped down. Then she suddenly became quiet and very weakly started calling, "Daddy, Daddy." The partition was open, so I kept telling her that I was there, and everything was going to be all right.

Since there was no children's psych ward at the local hospital, they took her to the emergency room. They rushed us right into a very small room where nurses hooked Brittany up to several monitors and busied themselves with taking her blood pressure and completing various and sundry other tasks. A doctor came in after fifteen minutes or so and asked Brittany how she was feeling and why she thought she was there. Sensing the answers necessary for her release, she naturally told him she felt fine, was okay now, and just wanted to go home.

Afterward he took Sheila and I outside and asked us what had happened. Sheila described how Brittany seemed not to be in control of her own thoughts and actions and was screaming, ranting and raving and trying to hurt herself and everyone else—but stopped short of theorizing about demonic possession. I said I felt we had been dealing with a demonic entity that had tried to possess Brittany.

"It might not have been quite as graphic and surreal as a scene from *The Exorcist*, but it came pretty close," I said. I told him that the only thing that seemed to keep the entity (as I openly referred to it) from completely taking over her body was when I sprinkled the holy water on her. He showed more interest in my theories than I thought he would, but that might only have been because he may have thought I was the one who was crazy. But whatever he may have theorized, he kept it to himself and said he was going to analyze the physical evidence and talk with a couple of other doctors about what steps should be taken next. We went back into the room to find Brittany much calmer and acting perfectly normal, though quite tired—as we all were.

The medical people weren't taking my stories about the powers of holy water too seriously, but I was certain that my old friend and parish priest, Father Jeff, would. Granted, we hadn't been attending church regularly for the last year or so—but I felt confident that I could still count on Father Jeff for anything. So as soon as we had finished with the doctor, I used the phone in the room to call him. Yes, Father Jeff would surely understand.

Sadly, however our priest did not react at all in the way I thought he would. I considered him a friend—not just our family priest. I was confident that once he heard the story of Brittany's possession, he'd rush down to the hospital to be by her side. However, after I'd given him the abbreviated version of the pure hell we'd gone through that night—he told me this was just an "area" that he didn't know anything about.

Although Father Jeff was an Episcopal priest, he had started his career as a Roman Catholic priest. He left the Catholic Church because he fell in love with a woman he met in a church organization for which he worked. Jane became his future wife. Because of his upbringing and education in Catholicism, I just assumed that all Catholic priests had at least some training in exorcisms. As a former Catholic myself, I knew that exorcism was an established rite of the Church. But my assumptions about Father Jeff's willingness to help were naive. He seemed very uncomfortable in even discussing what had happened to Brittany and said that he just couldn't drive the twenty miles or so to the hospital from his home that late. However he said that Jane was in the area and he'd tell her to stop by the hospital. I was quite disappointed at Father Jeff's cavalier attitude toward what I felt was a very real presence of evil threatening my family.

With that avenue of assistance closed to us, I grimly realized we were on our own. But thank God, Brittany had calmed down considerably over what we'd been dealing with earlier. We'd just spent over three hours dealing with some sort of foreign entity, speaking to it, holding it down, trying to prevent it from harming Brittany, i.e., banging her head against the floor or biting herself. But now she just seemed like a very tired and bewildered fifteen-year-old girl. She said she remembered what had happened, but it was as if she had been an observer rather than a participant.

But frankly, I wasn't convinced she was totally back in control of herself. Even though she was speaking much more sensibly, it still seemed to me that when she didn't think anyone was observing her directly, I'd catch her looking about the room as a prisoner might, formulating a plan of escape. At moments when Sheila and

I were talking to each other, out of the corner of my eye I'd notice Brittany with that dark glow I'd become familiar with as she thrashed about cursing all of creation on the floor of her pink ruffled room.

I also noticed that she'd be speaking normally with her mother and I one moment, but her mood would change dramatically when the occasional nurse would come in to check on her. She never actually said anything to the nurses that would cause them to suspect she wasn't herself, but I noticed that sharp, slightly squinting glare in her eyes I'd become so negatively familiar with as I wrestled with the entity. Her expression wasn't something you could exactly define, but I knew there was something off-kilter about it.

Jane arrived before long, sitting down next to Britt and holding her hand. As a licensed practical nurse, she was comfortable in dealing with just about any medical malady or physical situation. She talked for a few minutes with Brittany, asking her how she was feeling and expressing warmth and sympathy. But she kept her enquiries on a very superficial level. She never mentioned anything about possession or demonic entities.

Jane asked if she could pray with us, and Brittany tentatively said yes. I could see Britt wasn't particularly enthusiastic about receiving this prayer, but then she really hadn't been raised in a terribly religious home. Britt had been baptized into the Episcopal Church, but we only attended sporadically throughout most of her life.

We all joined hands around Brittany's bed and prayed a rather innocuous, nondescript prayer that made no mention of casting out demons or requesting protection from God against any kind of invasive evil. It certainly was well-intentioned and couldn't possibly have hurt—but it sure wasn't what I had been hoping for.

However, during the prayer I opened my eyes and looked over at Brittany. For a moment I had one of those blood-chilling moments you usually have only during nightmares. She was glaring at Jane with those dark eyes that just simply weren't hers. She or it silently glanced over at me, and on her face was a slight smirk, though it only lasted for a second. When she realized I was watching her, she closed her eyes again as the muscles in her face relaxed.

After the brief prayer, Sheila followed Jane out into the hallway, while I stayed with Brittany. Britt seemed back in control of her true personality now, but she was understandably exhausted. We all agreed that although we were fond of Jane, we had hoped to see Father Jeff. I volunteered that I was certain that he'd come by as soon as he could, but I could see that Brittany was extremely disappointed that he hadn't. Unfortunately, there was nothing to be done. Sheila returned after a few minutes followed by a nurse wanting to take Britt's blood pressure and do all the other mundane but necessary things the floor nurses are required to do every so often.

While the nurse attended to Brittany, Sheila motioned for me to follow her out into the hall. She said Jane had told her that Brittany "was not possessed" and suggested we have more psychiatric tests done and simply follow the doctors' recommendations. According to Jane, Brittany was experiencing symptoms of schizophrenia. We were both quite let down by this unemotional non-advice, but by then we were becoming numb to doctors, nurses, and now Jane not believing us.

About this time my mother arrived at the hospital. As we stood out in the hall, Mima showed me a letter she had found in Brittany's room. It was a suicide note. Now I felt like my sense of reality was being turned inside out. In the note, Brittany talked about how she could no longer cope with life, specifically referring to her recent breakup with Chase; apologized to everyone for being "a failure"; talked about her lifelong struggle with an up-and-down weight problem; and went on to conclude that her only course of action was to "end it all" by taking her own life. She didn't mention how she intended to accomplish her suicide.

I felt as if the floor had disappeared and left me standing on nothing. Brittany apparently was having serious issues that I was unaware of. I knew that she had been quite depressed since her breakup with Chase, but I was frankly flabbergasted that anyone would kill themselves over a teen romance. I did, however, remember that just about a week earlier, Brittany had watched a rented movie called *The Virgin Suicides* about a group of teen sisters who ended up committing suicide en masse—primarily over emotional issues. Brittany had always been extremely impressionable as well as dramatic, so I couldn't help but wonder if the influence of that movie wasn't at least partially responsible for the suicide note.

But the why of it seemed almost inconsequential at that particular moment. We were in a hospital because our daughter had been wheeled in after being tied down to a gurney, kicking and screaming from what appeared to me to be possession by some foreign entity. Was she truly suicidal? If so, was it due to emotional stress, or the influence of the entity I'd witnessed? But this was not a time for introspective navel-gazing. Our daughter's life was at stake, so there had to be a course of action. So when Mima went into the room to see Brittany, Sheila and I walked to the nurses' station and showed the letter to the nurse we'd gotten to know who took it to the attending ER doctor.

We had already been informed that all that could be done for Brittany was to hold her under observation, but the hospital near our home did not have a juvenile psych ward. At that point, the doctor was talking about sending her home and giving us a list of psychiatrists to call the next day for an appointment. However, the suicide note changed everything. I learned that night that any time an emotionally unstable patient is perceived to be a threat to his or her own life, extended observation is required. After seeing the letter, the doctor came out and told us they were going to call the two closest hospitals with juvenile psych wards to see what the bed availability was.

I did not want to see her placed in a psych ward, but I honestly also have to say that I was fearful of what might happen if I took her back home. I was completely worn out by then and had very little confidence that I could fight the demon or whatever this entity was again if it were to break out as soon as we got inside the door. The nurse came back and informed us that both juvenile wards downtown were currently full. The larger, more well-known facility was certain they wouldn't have an opening for several days—however, the smaller hospital was expecting a vacancy within a couple of hours. I couldn't decide whether this was welcome news or not, but there really wasn't time to ponder perceived possibilities. And yet I couldn't help but wonder that if Britt was receptive to malignant beings not existing in physical form nor encumbered by physical mass with the evil intent of possessing her body, would she be safe anywhere?

Sheila and I decided not to tell Brittany about the probable transfer to a psych ward until it was a certainty.

Britt was on her mother's insurance policy, so some hospital bureaucrat had finally cornered Sheila to fill out insurance forms. Trying to stay out of the way, I headed back to the small room. As I approached the door, Mima burst out in a dither, frantically looking right and left down the hall.

"Bill, go after Brittany," my mom shouted. "Stop her!"

"What do you mean? Where is she?" I rushed past Mima into the tiny room to find it empty with only the disheveled bed staring back at me.

"A nurse came in and told her to get ready," my mother said, "that they're transferring her to a children's psych ward. She jumped up, shoved me out of the way, got her coat, and ran out. She didn't even have her shoes on."

Before I could digest any of this and come up with an appropriate reaction, I saw a huge uniformed security guard coming around the corner with Brittany firmly in tow. She had gotten as far as the ER lobby before being nabbed. She was screaming that she wasn't going to another hospital and wanted to go home.

She was taken back to the room and strapped to the bed. The real Brittany seemed fully in charge now. She was bewildered by where she'd found herself and why she was shackled to the bed. It was a heart-wrenching experience to see my daughter overcome with fear, confusion, and tears.

Many years later I asked Brittany to write down what it was like for her during the possession. This is what she wrote.

Brittany's Possession Narrative

*I can safely tell you my brain was somewhere else for most of it.
I think it was kind of like when something traumatic happens to
you, your brain blocks it out.*

*However, I remember the burning feeling of holy water, and
then I woke up in a nightmare. I was strapped to the bed in a local hospital with my pastor's wife holding my hand. Apparently
we were waiting for me to be transferred to the local psych ward.
I kept crying, "Daddy? Mommy?" I could see them in the hallway.
I didn't want the pastor's wife there. She made the entities uneasy,
and every time she touched my hand I felt a shocking revulsion.*

Before long, orderlies and nurses came into the room and transferred the now self-aware Brittany to a gurney for transport to a hospital downtown with a juvenile psych ward. Mima went back home,
while Sheila and I followed the emergency vehicle to the new hospital. We were both apprehensive about this move, but we frankly
didn't know what else to do. I'll always fantasize if we might have
been better off if we'd just taken her home. But by that point, we
were both afraid that once Britt was away from professional help—
whatever had possessed her would come menacingly back, and
we'd already proven unable to cope with it.

Chapter 7
The Psych Ward

Once at the new hospital, Brittany was taken up to the juvenile psych ward while Sheila and I went to the office and filled out the admission papers. I knew she wasn't crazy, but there are no established remedies within the institutional frameworks of our society for anything as far-fetched as demonic possession. The questions the doctors and nurses asked us that night had nothing to do with the forces that had overcome our daughter—but I was grateful to at least have someone who was willing to help us.

As Britt was being checked into the ward, several medical personnel interviewed Sheila and me. I could tell from the look in their eyes that none of them believed us when we told them what had happened that night. The doctors' and nurses' explanation for Brittany's bizarre behavior on the night of the "holy water incident" was that she was simply insane.

After an hour or so, Sheila and I went home, leaving Brittany in the care of psychiatric doctors and nurses.

She was in the psych ward for slightly more than a week, and we visited her once a day. I discovered that unlike ordinary hospital visitations, you can't just drop in on a psych ward patient any time or sit with them for prolonged periods. Brittany was allowed to have visitors once a day for an hour. Although I tried to explain to them that she wasn't crazy, the visitation rules were inflexible. They were convinced she needed to be there for psychiatric reasons.

Sheila and I were at the hospital to visit Brittany each evening as permitted, and Mima visited at least every other day. Brittany seemed to be totally back to her old self upon those visits, and from her general demeanor, you'd never think anything as surreal as what we'd gone through that night could have possibly happened.

Mac Visits

I brought her brother, McCartney, to visit on a Sunday afternoon, after explaining to him what had happened and trying to prepare him as best I could. Mac was familiar with many of the paranormal experiences we had had at the house before the incident of Brittany's possession. He'd been there and had been introduced to the notion that such things were at least a part of reality.

Britt and McCartney grew up in different households, so their relationship wasn't *Brady Bunch* typical. Mac's mother and I split up when he was only six months old, so that six months was the only time they ever actually lived together. Upon Mac's visits every other week, sometimes they played together pretty well—but often they fought, more than I would have liked. Finally, by the time Britt was a teenager, they had started to get along much better. She had taken him under her wing and acted almost motherly toward Mac. In true little brother fashion, he really looked up to her.

I expected Brittany to rush up to Mac and hug him when she saw him at the hospital. However, that didn't go as I'd hoped. She was distant and withdrawn, with very little to say to him. I suppose this could be explained by embarrassment—after all, she was in a psych ward. But after a rather off-the-cuff hi and an unenthusiastic hug, she turned her attention to the food we'd brought and recounted to us how much she hated the place. She basically ignored her brother. I found that more than a bit troubling. I didn't know whether to shrug her complacency off as simply an unpleasant side effect of her incarceration or whether it was an indication that the entity was still in there. But regardless, I felt sorry for McCartney for just being brushed under the carpet.

Even by that point, I believe, the demonic entities were still exerting an influence.

Britt's Psych Ward Narrative

They transferred me to a local psych ward where Mom put a cross on my upper arm with a rubber band. It burned but kept them [the demonic entities] at bay—for the most part, anyway. I took the cross off to shower, and that was a bad move. I left the room in a towel, then threw a heavy lounge chair (that I should not have been able to pick up), tossing it like a ragdoll at one of my favorite counselors.

Searching for an Exorcist

Brittany would be coming home in a few days, so I felt like my number one priority was to arrange for some sort of cleansing: a deliverance or an exorcism. My first inclination was to go back to Father Jeff and implore him for help, but a phone call revealed that he was skeptical about there being any supernatural cause for Brittany's affliction based on the report that his wife Jane, the nurse, had given him.

"It's not within my level of expertise," he said.

Frankly, I was crushed. I had looked to Father Jeff for support and closure, but instead he was patronizing and condescending. Without putting it into so many words, I felt he was telling me I was crazy. He didn't say, "I don't believe in demons," but his attitude spoke volumes. Not only did he say this was out of his area of expertise, but he left me with the impression that he simply didn't believe such things happened in the real world. He showed no sympathy for our plight at all.

All this happened eighteen years ago, and it took me sixteen years before I stepped foot back inside another Episcopal church. Researching the liturgy and rites of the Episcopal faith, I learned that it does indeed have a rite of exorcism. The processes one would go through are slightly different than obtaining one in the Roman Catholic faith, but in a way are less complicated. If an Episcopal priest feels that an exorcism is warranted, he/she refers the case to the bishop of that diocese. If the bishop agrees an exorcism is needed to expel demonic entities, then the bishop is the one who performs it.

I have struggled with Father Jeff's lack of concern all these years. But perhaps he wasn't simply being callous. Perhaps he was just scared, but that's no excuse. After what I had seen that night, I was scared too. But I couldn't let that stop me.

Next, I tried appealing to the local Catholic diocese. After summarizing my plight over the phone to a secretary, I was transferred to a priest who civilly heard me out but then politely informed me that the Catholic process for being granted an exorcism was extremely complicated and involved. There were so many layers of bureaucracy to weed through even to be granted a hearing. He also didn't feel like this whole matter was within his area of expertise. That sounded familiar. At least he was honest enough to confide that if I were in any hurry at all, the Catholic diocese wouldn't be able to help me.

When the Catholic diocese declined, I was at a loss as to what to do. Brittany was at least safe as long as she was in the hospital, but once she was released, I was convinced an exorcism was the only solution—or all hell would break loose again.

I started thinking about stocking up on more holy water, because it was the only thing that the entity had recoiled from. I had gotten the holy water from my friend Ann. She got it at her church from a Greek Orthodox priest.

I called Ann and told her about the possession and how her holy water had been the only thing that helped. By now I had become used to people treating me as if I were crazy, but she was very sympathetic. She suggested I talk to the Greek Orthodox priest at her church and gave me his number. I called the priest up and gave him a synopsis of the events of the last few weeks. After my lack of luck with these Episcopal and Catholic churches, I was a bit surprised to hear the sympathy in his voice. He didn't act like he thought I had lost my mind or that I was actually from Mars. He agreed to meet with me at his home. For the first time since it all started, I began to have hope.

Father Nicholas lived in a small Tudor bungalow near his church. He was emotionally warm and sympathetic, but at the same time I could tell this was a no-nonsense kind of guy. He informed me that the Greek Orthodox Church did indeed have a rite of exorcism, that he had witnessed cases of possession himself, and in no way did he deny my assertions. But then he proceeded to outline the conditions for his services. He described how modern teenagers often were preyed upon by demonic spirits because of the evils of the lyrics in the rock 'n' roll music they listened to. Suddenly my hopes for a resolution to our dilemma came crashing down. He went on to say that he would conduct an exorcism only if my family was willing to begin attending his church.

In his concept of ultimate reality, this was the only way the devil could be kept at bay. The exorcism that I knew Brittany absolutely had to have seemed to be slipping through my fingers, because I knew that my family simply couldn't be who Father Nicholas wanted us to become. Although there was much of modern rock 'n' roll music I didn't care for myself, I didn't agree that it was inherently evil. I also knew that for any exorcism to work, the subject (in this case, Brittany) had to have faith in the exorcist. Brittany was never going to exhibit faith in someone who was telling her she had to give up her favorite style of music. So I knew a Greek Orthodox exorcism was not in the cards. I was polite and thanked him for his time and said I would call him, knowing that I wouldn't. I was relieved I'd finally found someone who believed my story, but also despondent because I'd just gone down another dead-end street.

I had just about run out of options. On the trip home, it occurred to me to call my old friend Joel (the director of the Bell Witch play Brittany had done several months earlier). He was very fond of Brittany, a dear friend, and a trusted adviser. I filled him in on everything that had happened to us in the last few weeks. He was stunned. Joel didn't question my story for a second. All his adult life he had been interested in the paranormal, though he had never personally known anyone who had been face-to-face with what my family had encountered recently. I filled him in on my frustration with the total lack of success I'd had in finding someone to perform an exorcism on Brittany.

Joel agreed with me that there was not a minute to lose in securing the assistance of an authority on demonic possessions. He asked if I'd ever heard of the noted demonologists who were among the first paranormal investigators of the Amityville haunting case. I had no idea who they were, though I'd seen a movie about it years earlier. But I trusted Joel. He loaned me a couple of books written by them about demonic possession, giving examples from various cases they had worked on.

I wasted no time in getting their email address off their website and sent a frantic plea to them asking for help, advice, or whatever they could do to assist. I sent them an attachment of my account of the possession along with my email begging for help. I didn't know whether to expect an answer or not, but I seemed to have no other choices.

I received an email the next morning. One of the demonologists answered, essentially saying that she was very sympathetic with my family's plight and thought that we may very likely have a valid case of demonic possession going on. However, her husband was having health problems at the time. She was going to pass along my information to her trusted assistant and nephew. She gave me his phone number and suggested I call him. I sent her an email thanking her, saying I'd be calling her assistant very soon.

I wanted to give him time to look over the material his aunt had supplied him with, but I didn't really have time to spare. After a few hours, I called him. He was extremely compassionate and sympathetic. He had read the journal I'd kept of the night of the possession, and he said that it certainly sounded to him like there was the possibility of a valid case. But his organization received many calls for assistance and they could only respond to a limited number. His group could not afford to send down a team of investigators from Connecticut with an expensive plethora of sensitive, technical detection equipment for free. I admitted that I was just a poor newspaper editor and couldn't afford to pay them. He also said that even if money were not a consideration, he couldn't assemble a team and get down to Nashville for several months—and it sounded to him as if I needed someone right then.

But again, he was very sympathetic and said he had a suggestion that could be as effective as anything his group could do anyway. He said that many major American cities had local psychics, paranormal investigative groups, and demonologists. Growing up in the Nashville area, I was less sure about its ability to attract such freethinking urbanites. But he had me thinking about solutions I hadn't previously considered—solutions that were right under my nose.

Over the last few years I had become acquaintances and even friends with a number of psychics who called Nashville home—primarily from editing a paranormal magazine. I don't know why I didn't think of it immediately, but it took this one man's prompting to make me realize that my old friend Laurel just might be the key. She had been a major fixture of the Nashville metaphysical community for years. Laurel would know what to do.

I thanked him for his time and wise advice. He wished me the best, assuring me that he was sure God would take good care of my daughter.

As soon as I got off the phone with him, I called Laurel and recounted the story of Brittany's possession.

I filled her in on everything that had happened from the first night of the possession through my attempts to procure a priest. I'm sure my friend sensed the desperation in my voice; she was not only sympathetic but also cool and collected. Laurel asked detailed questions and didn't seem in the least bit skeptical. After patiently listening to my recounting of our emotional trek through a demonic Sinai, I asked her if she knew of anyone in our area who could perform an exorcism.

"Sure, me," she replied simply but confidently.

She said that she had done a number of exorcisms (or cleansings) in the past and was more than familiar with the process. I asked if she could possibly visit Brittany in the hospital beforehand, but she was scheduled to go out of town the next day to speak at a Unity church in Georgia. A major part of Laurel's work involved traveling all over the United States giving metaphysical lectures and psychic readings to various groups. But although she wouldn't be able to get out of this previous engagement, Laurel had a friend named Lisa who assisted in her exorcisms. She asked me if I'd mind if Lisa dropped by to see Brittany—mostly just to get to know her and make friends. I thought that was a great idea, gave Laurel the visitation hours, and discussed the logistics of the upcoming exorcism. It seemed that Laurel wasn't scheduled to return to Nashville until the day after Brittany was set to be released. We both agreed that the exorcism needed to occur as soon as Britt came home. I honestly feared that whatever had possessed her would come back and be ready for a rematch.

Since Laurel couldn't change the date of her return, that meant I had to get Britt's release date postponed a day or two. We would have to get Brittany's primary psychiatrist to petition the insurance company to extend her stay an additional night—not such a big deal at the time. Back in 2001, doctors had a bit more latitude in saying when a patient could be released from the hospital than they do today. We just had to convince her psychiatrist that Britt needed to stay an extra day. How was I going to ask him to extend her stay another night on the grounds of fitting into the timetable of my exorcist? Especially since he didn't believe my story about demonic possession anyway.

Dr. Happy

None of the medical professionals I'd talked to during this ordeal had taken my assertion of demonic possession seriously. The official diagnosis was a hodgepodge of possibles: possible schizophrenic; possible bipolar; possible multiple personality disorder; possible psychosis. No psychiatric "-osis" had been determined upon, and demonic possession wasn't even in the running as a possibility. But I knew that I was going to have to play the game in order to get Brittany out of the psychiatric unit so she could get the exorcism I was hoping would free her.

Our nickname for Brittany's psychiatrist was "Dr. Happy." I think he was the most preposterously optimistic person I have ever met. My family had just gone through the most horrible, traumatic event we could ever possibly have conceived. Dr. Happy ignored virtually everything we tried to tell him about what had actually happened to Brittany during the night of the possession as if it were irrelevant. He was also frustratingly skeptical when we told him there had been no signs of her displaying psychological or emotional trauma of any kind prior to that night. He was absolutely and stalwartly convinced that her eventual breakdown was simply the culmination of years of psychological abnormality building to a crescendo and finally erupting that night. We called him Dr. Happy because he chatted on incessantly about plans for Britt's rejuvenation and impending total recovery after his proposed program of therapy—ignoring what we were telling him based on face-to-face observations. To Sheila and me, he seemed oblivious to the real world we were trying to describe. How could he make her better if he insisted on denying what had really happened to her? Ultimately, we just went along with him, realizing that resistance was futile.

They had tested and observed Brittany for a week and wanted her to continue to come in for outpatient observation during the day for an additional week. We made up a story about how my mother wouldn't be able to stay with Brittany until the day *after* she was scheduled for release. Sheila and I both worked, so my mom would have been the only one who could watch her. However, Dr. Happy didn't seem to care. He denied our request and said the previously scheduled release would stand. This was a crushing blow, but there just didn't seem to be anything we could do about it. Sheila and I stopped by to see Brittany before we left the hospital to give her the bad news. She was very upset and started crying. She didn't want to take the chance of going through another night of being haunted by demons any more than we did. We tried to explain that we'd bring her home, and then she could see Laurel the next day.

Because of the unit's regulations, we were only allowed to be with Brittany for a few minutes and had to leave. She was still crying and frankly distraught. We told her to ask to speak with Dr. Happy herself. Maybe he would listen to her where he hadn't to us. The three of us went to the nurses' desk, and through her tears, Brittany told them she wanted to have the doctor contact her. Up till that time, I hadn't been too impressed with the compassion I'd seen from the staff—but this particular nurse showed real concern, called Dr. Happy's office, and said they promised he would stop by that night and talk to her. Finally, it seemed that someone was showing genuine concern. Britt was placated and stopped sobbing. Sheila and I left, promising to come see her the next morning regardless of the doctor's decision. It truly broke my heart to leave her. She had been so positive and enthusiastic about receiving Laurel's help that watching her hopes dashed (even temporarily) was tough. Brittany had come to trust and even love Laurel over the years, and the possibility of Laurel helping her had been the only factor giving her any hope at all. Neither Sheila or I had any real hope that Dr. Happy would relent and change his mind at the insistence of a mere patient, so we went ahead and made plans to pick Britt up the next day.

However there were still a few silver linings in the sullen, gray cloud that had engulfed us. Dr. Happy was sufficiently moved by Britt's plea, and postponed her release from the hospital until the next day. I'm still not sure what she told him to make him change his mind, and after all these years she doesn't remember. But I guess it just goes to prove that there was at least a little warmth in the good doctor after all. The pleas of a frightened young girl had worked. Sheila would take Britt back and forth for her week of outpatient therapy, but the hurdle of scheduling the exorcism to fit with Laurel's return to town had been overcome. So after about a week in the juvenile psych ward, she was allowed to come home.

Chapter 8
The Exorcism

That afternoon, Laurel and her assistant Lisa had cleansed both houses with sage and prayers—much like Laurel had cleansed my friends' home a year earlier. Nothing spooky or dramatic— mostly just prayers of protection and blessing that would have been acceptable to any religion. Lisa followed Laurel around both houses waving the fragrant, misty sage and that was that.

Shortly after we got home and started eating dinner, Laurel and Lisa arrived. Soon the ordeal would begin.

Most of this information came directly from a journal I kept at the time of the possession. But the exorcism itself proved to be such an exhausting and overwhelming ordeal that I did not write it down immediately.

However, about three weeks afterward, I got together with Laurel and she made a tape of her recollections of the event. Most of the following description comes directly from her taped narra- tive. These references will be noted as such.

The Release

Brittany came into the living room and Laurel had her sit down in a chair in the middle of the room, with me, Laurel, and Lisa sitting on the sofa in front of her. Sheila was seated in a chair near the stairwell maybe six feet to Britt's right. Mima was sitting on the stairs behind Sheila.

Brittany said, "Alright, I'm ready," and the process began. Laurel told her to just relax and sit back. She began the ceremony by gently inviting any entity or entities that might be residing inside Brittany to leave her and "return to the light."

Britt seemed to fall unconscious for a second as her head slumped to one side. When her eyes opened, she had this wide-eyed look on her face like she was seeing the room for the first time.

"Hello," she said as she cocked her head jauntily and looked from one of us to the other. She had a mischievous, even evil grin on her face.

Laurel again invited the entity to leave Brittany and return to the light.

"I don't think so," it replied. With that, Brittany arose and walked toward the kitchen, surveying everything as if she'd never seen any of it before—even though we'd lived in the condo over five years by then. Although her attitude was inquisitive, she also seemed to be in somewhat of a hurry. By the time she reached the door leading into the kitchen, I came up behind her.

"Where do you think you're going?" I asked.

"You don't need to know everything," it answered. She quickly walked to the counter where the cutlery is kept and began opening the drawer.

"We don't need anything in there," I said as I stopped her by grasping her wrist. She turned to me, growling like an animal and struggled to free her hand. But I held both her wrists, and by then Sheila and Laurel had joined us. Brittany was now kicking, screaming, and hissing. But I had learned my lesson from the first episode of possession. Since Brittany was no longer in control of her own faculties, she (or rather, the entity) would be trying to harm herself or others unless she was totally restrained. So with the entity flailing, kicking, and raging to any within earshot that it would kill us as well as Brittany—Sheila, Laurel, and I wrestled her to the ground with the prime objective being to prevent her from hurting herself.

"They didn't initially struggle against anyone [in particular]," Laurel said on the tape. "The only struggle against us was because we were holding her down."

As we held Britt down, one entity after another came to the surface and attempted to assert itself. Laurel was always respectful of them—although firm in her demands that they release their hold on Brittany.

"We started in the kitchen with a bunch of releases," Laurel continued on the tape. "What I was doing was seeking to identify ways to release each specific entity or groups of entities as they came up."

Laurel often called upon other friendly entities with whom the entity possessing Brittany would be familiar. Laurel could psychically perceive spirits these possessing entities might recognize and thus enlisted their help by allowing them to channel through her. As I held Brittany's hands and Sheila straddled her to hold down her legs, Laurel crouched over Britt and spoke to her in voices and accents not her own, trying to convince these entities to leave our daughter and go to the light.

Not all of the entities possessing Brittany seemed to be evil. In fact, many of them were quite pleasant, entertaining, and even funny. When one of these would come through, the evil look would pass from Brittany's face and a look of innocent, wide-eyed incredulity would emerge. Occasionally, one of these nice entities would not seem to have a working command of the English language.

More than once, Laurel spoke in response to some unrecognizable foreign language with which the entities possessing Brittany wanted to communicate. The first such incident happened as Brittany began speaking in some unknown foreign tongue. It was more than a bit eerie to watch this exchange between Laurel and the fifteen-year-old on the floor being possessed by disembodied spirits. The entity speaking through Brittany would often seem amazed that Laurel (or the entity channeling through her) could speak its language. Then they would begin chattering away. Being involved in theatre, I can do a wide array of foreign dialects, and can recognize most of the standard European languages as such when I hear them. However, the languages being parlayed between Laurel and Brittany must have been ancient, archaic ones no longer in everyday use. Or as Laurel explained later, some of them were even extraterrestrial.

A good deal of the releasing went on in the kitchen. However, after an hour or so, Brittany regained control of her body. She was exhausted, but I helped her up and we went back into the living room.

"Much was happening with Brittany," Laurel said on the tape. "There were the entities, and lots of screaming and anger from them was coming out. I did not experience superhuman strength coming from them, or if I did, the guides were giving me the superhuman strength to counter it."

I might add that in this de-possessing, unlike others Laurel had held, she had Sheila and I to help hold the subject down. So Brittany may not have seemed as strong to Laurel as she really was, but it was taking three grown adults to hold this 5' 4", 135 lb. teenager down.

"The entities found out early on in the process that the three of us were physically a match for them," Laurel continued, "and that they could not simply become destructive and hurt all of us, including and especially Brittany. As a matter of fact, I told some friends afterward about the process, and I said it gave me a new appreciation for my weight and bulk. There is value in this.

"I went through the releasing process that I usually do," she continued. "I start with what I call the lightweights, the collections of church mice. I do affirmations; I do invitations to come to the light—and I almost immediately started getting this energy sensation. This tells me the energy is moving. So the little ones in there were going, 'Oh my God! It's coming down! Head for the hills!' And they're taking off, which is what we were going for. So we started releasing the little ones with this invitation:

"'Dear ones, welcome in love and light. You are healed and forgiven, redeemed and restored. You are not now, nor were you ever truly a part of darkness. You are now filled with your own higher consciousness, your light self.' And I believe I said 'your Christself,' knowing it would be more acceptable under that situation. 'You are filled with the love of the universe (and I may have said Christ instead of universe). Go in peace, go in peace, go in peace.'

"So at that point the little ones, who were more or less by-standers anyway, were going, 'Yeah, I'll go ... I'm ready!'

"When the nice ones came through, we didn't attempt to re-strain them. It was easy to tell which ones were friendly and which ones were malevolent. With the wicked ones, even if they were smiling and sounded friendly, you could feel a tension in Brittany's body—like a cat ready to pounce."

Frequently, these nice entities would get up and wander about the house. At the time we had two cats, Spot and Baby, who were considerably startled by one entity that said it was from a land cov-ered by water. As the aquatic entity, Brittany would utter this high-pitched cross between a scream and a squeal that sounded very much like the sound you hear porpoises make. This entity could not communicate in English, but unlike many of the others, it was quite good at communicating with gestures, nods of the head, and humming sounds that would indicate approval or disapproval. It seemed to basically understand us but could not manipulate vocal communication itself. Perhaps it was picking up thoughts rather than understanding words.

The aquatic entity possessing Britt began walking up the steps and totally freaked when it saw a large stuffed fish at the top of the landing. I have a five-foot-long El Dorado fish mounted that my fa-ther caught when I was a little boy. The aquatic entity became hys-terical when it saw the El Dorado. I gently tried to explain what it was, and that I was not the one who had killed it. Nevertheless, the entity was inconsolable until I promised I'd take it down. With sweeping gestures, it demanded I remove the fish from the wall at that precise moment, but I said that was not convenient considering everything else that was going on and promised to take it down later. This seemed to placate it, so Britt (as the aquatic entity) went about inspecting the rest of the house. Eventually, she sat down at the foot of her bed. Britt seemed to pass out and slumped down onto the bed. About a second went by, then Brittany returned as herself and asked me how she got into her bedroom, and then we returned downstairs. After a short break, we continued.

When Britt went back into her trance state, Sheila and I were again holding her down not knowing what or who would surface next. Laurel began the invitation again, beseeching any remaining entities to exit.

"Then I went to the next level," Laurel continued on the tape, "which is to say: 'You have nothing to fear. The light doesn't hurt. You will not be punished. You will not be sent to hell. You will be comforted, counseled, guided, and loved. This is your opportunity to get the help you need. I know there are some of you in there who don't want to be dead. Well, that's tough. You are dead! Here's your chance to no longer be wandering endlessly, earthbound.'

"Then we went immediately to round three," she said, "which is for the heavyweights. I began by saying to them: 'I say to you exactly what I said to the others. I know you think of yourselves as bad dudes and all that. And that's okay. But I say to you, welcome in love and light. You are healed and forgiven. It's time to come home.'"

Laurel said she identified three kinds of darkness hiding within Brittany. She said this was in addition to spirits of those who may have gotten stuck on this planet visiting here on a fact-finding mission and became separated from their party, and then didn't get home.

First Dark Entity Type: Inverted Light

"These cases are dealt with differently," Laurel said, "but of those trying to be *bad*, there are three types. The first is called inverted light.

"These are dark angels. They are beings of light who are playing the role of villain on stage to create the duality process in the universe. Darkness is necessary for light to push against. Dark angels were actually just part of the learning process in our struggle for eventual perfection and reunification with the Godhead. Not innately evil, they were simply playing a part. However, somewhere along the way they started buying into their own PR. They began believing the wickedness they merely performed was real. They are beings of light. They always were. They always will be merely playing the dark role.

"In the depossession process, we approach them with certain code phrases, such as: 'It is the Age of Completion.'

"'Your promise is kept. There will always be a way home.' At that point, we enter into a dialogue with the entity. They tell me psychically or through the subject what problems may arise in the release. There may be tangled energy somewhere in the subject's body, for example. I tell them about going home to the planet of light, after which (if they wish) they may return and work as beings of light not darkness—and often they do. They frequently volunteer to help. Such was the case with the entity we came to know as Spence."

Spence

After Laurel released four or five of the dark beings and a number of the little ones, an entity calling itself Kalikalik began speaking through Brittany. At first it spoke in some unknown language that I didn't recognize; however, soon he and Laurel were conversing freely in the mysterious tongue. After seeing the looks of confusion on our faces, Laurel asked the entity if it would speak in English so others could understand. It then spoke with a perfectly gentlemanly Irish accent, admonishing Sheila and I that it wasn't necessary to hold him down. He said he was there to help. Laurel recognized him as one of the dark beings she had dealt with before. She said he had "returned to the light" and now worked on earth as a sort of messenger helping people. He told us he was Brittany's guardian angel and asked us to call him Spence, a name he had gone by in a life as an incarnated human being.

Spence told us the evil ones had Brittany in a dark place and wouldn't let her out. He said she couldn't see us, and for all she knew she'd never come back again. He said there were upside-down crucifixes, fire, and beings there for no other purpose than to scare her into thinking that all was hopeless. Laurel asked him to go to her and tell her that everything would soon be okay and that we were in the process of removing all the dark ones. He was gone for maybe half a minute. Meanwhile, Brittany looked as though she were asleep. Spence then returned, said that he'd told her she was very frightened, and begged us to hurry.

Laurel then asked Spence if he could "take a look" and see how many entities were left inside Brittany. This only took a split second. He returned saying that the total number of entities either possessing or hiding within her had been seventeen dark entitles and over a thousand little ones. Laurel had expelled five of the dark ones. Several hundred of the little ones had left en masse in several different groups. He said he would try to gather more groups together and escort them out. He also said he could help expel the dark ones, but we'd have to be rigorously involved in that process.

As Spence left again, Brittany began speaking in a tiny little voice. It identified itself by some name I'd never heard and can't recall. It informed us it was a fairy and had been with Brittany since she was a toddler. The fairy described how it used to sit and play with Britt and loved her toys. Laurel assured her it was safe to leave and called upon entities with whom the fairy was familiar to help in the transition. Laurel asked if she knew an angel named Kalikalik or Spence.

"Oh yes, he's nice," the fairy replied.

Laurel then asked if the fairy would go with him; she said yes and that she'd wait until he came to collect her.

Spence returned and said one of the dark ones was trying to come out and he couldn't hold it at bay much longer. Laurel assured him that this was all right and to let it out.

"Hold her down then," Spence said. Still possessing Brittany, Spence gently leaned back, asked for a pillow (several, in fact), and relaxed. "Here he comes," said Spence in his Irish accent. "Goodbye."

With that, Brittany started snarling and growling, spitting, cursing, and trying to break away from the hold that Sheila, Laurel, and I had on her. Laurel utilized several positive affirmations to invoke the entity to leave of its own free will.

Britt's Narrative of the Exorcism

I remember my parents bringing me pepperoni pizza the night they took me home. Then came the exorcism. A trusted friend (Laurel, who has since passed) came to the house. I don't really know, but I guess it was your typical exorcism. I remember evil coursing through my veins during the pre-performance period before Laurel got started with the exorcism. I sucked up those nasty, evil feelings and tried to just relax.

The exorcism commenced, and the rest is totally foggy. But I remember the evil entities showing me my own funeral and having to have a closed casket because I died with a look of horror the funeral director couldn't fix. When they showed me that, I fought as hard as I could to get to the surface—to tell them I was fighting. My parents sang me a favorite childhood song [probably "Dixie"] to keep me conscious. Then, after nine long excruciating hours, the evil was gone—or so I thought at the time.

Second Dark Entity Type: Luciferic or Anormonic Darkness

Laurel continued on the tape, describing the different kinds of dark entities:

"This is the beast, the biblical beast. This is a non-humanoid, non-angelic darkness. I tell them that I really don't care what their motives are; their tenure here on earth has come to an end. When we find them, we say something like, 'Your key member has already been shipped back to the home planet. Then we made an arrangement in case we found some more of you out there. Now there is a beam for you to ride home. You have two choices: Get on it and go, or I'll squish you like a bug.'"

Laurel said this kind of darkness is not known for its willingness to cooperate, but "generally they look at the offer, check it out, and read my memory files. Then generally they say 'Oh yeah, they sent him home. Well, we're going home too.'"

Spence warned us that the approaching Luciferian entity was going to be a bad one, and he was definitely right. Although the three of us were holding Brittany down as firmly as possible, it was still all we could do to keep her still. The snarling, growling, and hissing was intense. Laurel spoke her affirmations, but it just scoffed. Sheila held a cross to Brittany's forehead, and although this seemed to cause the demon a good deal of pain, it wasn't about to let up. It started telling us that Brittany would never resurface, following this up with dire threats directly aimed at us.

I was so mad by this point that my natural sarcasm began to surface. I remember after one particularly vile threat, I said something to the effect of: "Attention, K-Mart shoppers, attention—badass dude on aisle three. Everyone tremble and shake." To which it replied, "Oh, you're the funny one, aren't you?" just before spitting in my face. My sarcasm was inappropriate, but sometimes that's just how I react to stress. I had learned enough from Laurel, though, to know that the best way to fight one of these things was with love and kindness. It was best to just hold it, but not fight back. When it snarled and spit in my face, I leaned over and gently kissed my daughter's forehead. This seemed to have about the same effect the holy water had had in the initial incident two weeks earlier. She writhed as if in pain and growled.

I realized at that moment the greatest weapon with which to fight these fiends was simply love.

The entity began speaking in Laurel's direction in one of those odd languages. Laurel replied in a similar tongue. The entity then replied more angrily, and Brittany's head shook violently. I asked what had been transpiring. Laurel replied that she had given it an ultimatum, telling it she would count to ten, and if it didn't come out, she would press her crystal to Brittany's forehead, effectively obliterating the entity.

Lisa came forward with a crystal and challenged the entity to do as Laurel had bid it. Laurel began counting to ten. Since all the other dark entities had begrudgingly exited, I fully expected this one to pull out also, no matter how obstinate it had initially seemed.

It didn't. Laurel's count reached ten, and the entity essentially dared her to keep her threat. Snarling and spitting worse than ever, the entity seemed self-assured that Laurel wouldn't follow through. After asking it to leave peacefully one more time and receiving nothing more than yet another growl, Laurel simply said alright and pressed the crystal to Brittany's forehead as she called upon some deity with whom the possessing entity was familiar. Lisa then utilized a different type crystal, which she also pressed to Brittany's forehead.

When the entity recognized the deity Laurel had called upon, a look of shock and terror spread across Britt's face. The entity bucked and lurched forward with renewed strength. Brittany screamed a throaty retort and was then silent. She appeared to have passed out. I hugged her and kissed her forehead. Her mother also embraced Brittany. Within a few moments, our daughter returned to consciousness as herself and asked for a drink. Mima got her a Dr. Pepper, Britt's favorite.

"What happened there?" I asked Laurel.

"When he refused to leave, I made good on my promise. I utterly annihilated him just like I told him I would. I don't like to do that, and usually you don't have to. But it was the only way I could prove to this one and the others still in there that we mean business."

Later Laurel described the third kind of darkness to me but said that this was not a type of entity she found in Brittany.

Third Dark Entity Type: Animal Dark

"When spirit is given to newly born human beings, sometimes the spark of divinity most of us get doesn't lock in," Laurel said. She said the God light is missing from these individuals. They may be brilliant, but they have zero understanding or zero caring for the harm they may cause to others.

"But I see that generally in people," Laurel said. "I don't normally see that in spiritual entities. Animal dark was not an issue when we were working with Brittany. My task while we were holding Brittany down was to either persuade or force (preferably persuade) the entities to leave her. And to leave her in such a way that they wouldn't just be hanging out in the house waiting for a chance to hop back on. You see, I can get them off of a subject relatively easily. But that doesn't solve the problem on a continuing basis.

"Any entities that trouble her from that point on won't be the same ones," Laurel continued. "The ones we dealt with are gone. I would name names that might mean nothing to you, but the entities would recognize them. They might say, 'Yes, I know him. Yes, if he'll help me, then sure, I'll go with him.' The guides provide someone that the entity can trust. Sometimes some of them are afraid to come out.

"Well, we got several dark entities off in the first round. And then we came up with these darling little fairy-like beings who were friendly and gave us some information. One said she had been inside Brittany since she was three years old, and another spirit was a little girl in a pretty yellow dress who died in the late 1800s. These fairies were scared of the bad ones. So we had to negotiate releases of them in several groups. We brought people in, Mother Mary, notably, to help the little ones feel safe so they could transfer.

"At that point we had to convince Brittany, the real Brittany inside there somewhere, that it was safe to let these little ones go. She had cared for them for a long time as we discovered, and it was not easy for her to let them go. For one thing, she would be lonely without them. This is typical of any releases, including the ones that are not like full-blown manifestations of a violent situation. So we got a bunch of them out, and then we did another round of bad ones. Then the one we now know as Spence, Kalikalik, came through, and I recognized his energy. I asked him if he was Kalikalik. He replied yes, and then he would tell us how many were left of the bad ones and of the good ones or the ones being sheltered.

"There were over a thousand of the sheltering ones. We would move them out in batches. There was one bad one who wouldn't cooperate, and we had to annihilate him. Annihilation is where the personality is truly destroyed; the energy goes back to pure energy, and there is nothing left. We gave him a choice, and he didn't take it. I'd rather they move out more or less peacefully, and thankfully we only had to squish one.

"Then occasionally Brittany would come up and would want comfort from you. This worked fine. Your instincts were great.

You were very good about remembering that that was your kid's body, with a minimal amount of force to hold her down."

Jezebel

Toward the end of the cleansing or exorcism session, one of the dark ones claimed to be the legendary temptress Jezebel. She was a particularly nasty one who claimed she "knew Jesus" in the biblical sense. She engaged Sheila directly, claiming she "recognized another whore" when she saw one. Laurel challenged Jezebel, saying they had been sisters in a previous life. There was a good bit of heated exchange between Laurel and Jezebel, them having engaged on this ethereal plane before.

Laurel tried to reason with her, inviting her to return to the light. This was the first demonic figure that I had any compassion for. Up until this particular one, I had been having a bit of trouble understanding why Laurel cared whether they returned to the light or not. Just squish them all and be done with it. However, with Jezebel it was different for some reason. I was feeling actual compassion for this wicked, demonic being inhabiting my only daughter. It suddenly became clear to me why Laurel was showing compassion to these dark entities and inviting them to return to the God source, free of punishment, instead of annihilating them.

When Jezebel finally came around and accepted the love Laurel was offering her, I actually felt a bit warm inside and started to well up. Brittany, as Jezebel, began crying. Then she and Laurel hugged and promised never to become estranged as sisters again. Then Britt fell back, and Jezebel was gone as quickly as she had come.

Provocation and Physical Struggle

At one point, one of the dark entities began taunting Sheila, saying some very negative personal things in an effort to provoke her. The entity and Sheila eventually got into a real shouting match. Then it spit in Sheila's face, and in a fit of anger, Sheila spit in Brittany's face. Sheila became so provoked by the entity that she raised her hand as if to strike Brittany in the face.

"I suggested that Sheila back off," Laurel continued, "because the conflict might have been, among other things, a mother-daughter conflict that was not productive for either of them—and certainly was not productive for the releasing process. I complemented Sheila afterward for cooperating and backing off when I asked her to.

"The closer we came to having the heavyweights removed, the more we were dealing with Kalikalik [Spence, as you know him], and the more the real problems in Brittany's life started to surface. We were getting down to the point where it was Brittany's own genuine anger.

"Now from my point of view, I should tell you that this release was not unlike other releases I've done. Except for one thing, and that was the client. The subject was fighting physically. Except for that, it was just what I've done for hundreds and hundreds of people. I don't regret the fight, and I would encourage you not to regret the fight—because I really don't think that either Sheila or Brittany would have accepted the release, or the fact that the work was done, that the job got done, if there hadn't been a physical struggle.

The Use of Crystals

I asked Laurel to explain the use of crystals during the cleansing. I commented on how the various entities seemed to recoil to the touch of the crystals as if being burned. She explained that they function in much the same way as the holy water I had used during the first night. Crystals can draw out negativity, and that actually hurts the entity.

"We did use the crystals to absorb some of the negativity and to help force it out," she said.

More Than a Little "Draining"

The whole release/exorcism process took six hours, from 8:30 p.m. to 2:30 a.m. We chatted with Spence, through Brittany, for about another hour afterward. Britt, Sheila, Mima, and I then thanked and hugged Laurel and Lisa and said our goodbyes. They left about 3:30 a.m. It was a grueling six hours, and I really hadn't expected it to last that long; although I've read since about exorcisms that took even longer.

"It was physically demanding, and everyone was exhausted," Laurel said. "On the whole, I thought Brittany did absolutely beautifully."

Although the victim and the exorcist are the focus of any exorcism, this one at least had a supporting cast: "You and Sheila were great," Laurel said, "comforting her when she was Brittany, with an appropriate response to the entities, depending on who we were talking to."

Physically, I didn't feel normal for several days. I can only imagine how my eighty-year-old mother felt. But Mima hung in there. She was there with us till the bitter end. On numerous occasions she went back and forth (between entities) to the kitchen to bring water for Laurel, Sheila, Lisa, and me, and Dr. Pepper for her granddaughter.

Lisa seemed to be mostly there for moral support and maybe to learn. Laurel had brought a cinched velvet bag in which she kept crystals with various spiritual purposes. Occasionally, she requested a specific crystal and Lisa dutifully supplied it.

Laurel's Estimation of Spence

The "Spence" entity would come in and out of Britt's life for the next decade and a half. She continued to channel him sporadically long after the exorcism. For years, Spence might pop up anytime, anywhere—usually at inconvenient times. For many years, I often pondered just what exactly he is. Fallen angel? Past-life personality? Alter ego? Interdimensional traveler?

"Now as far as Spence is concerned, it would probably be true to say that he is an alter ego of Brittany in addition to being an angel. It appears to me that speaking as Spence with the Irish accent gives her a chance to say things that she perhaps is not comfortable in saying, or to discuss her own conflicts or her own fears about what is happening in her life. But Spence is echoing Brittany's fear. And as that, I do see him as a separate being, as Kalikalik, who was one of those whom I first met as a dark being, a dark angel (the energy is what I recognized). But he returned to the light and volunteered to be a helper."

I asked her if he was a combination of a separate entity and an alter ego.

"I think he is an actual entity," Laurel replied, "that she has a long-ago connection to and contact with. I think he is allowing her to express herself through him, and that's how you get the alter ego part.

"Brittany really needs to know that she's in charge of her own body and her own life—that no entity, no dark spirit, no fallen angel, no critter from outer space, nothing, can make her do anything. They cannot force her. They cannot take her consciousness away from her in order to come through her. But if they convince her that they are more powerful—she buys into it, and then it happens."

Taking Control

Laurel went on to describe the importance of understanding how we are all in control of our own consciousness—and the importance the God force within each of us plays in mastering that control. I think this may very well be the most important thing in this book. For anyone out there battling the possession of any kind of alien entity—please, take this to heart:

"Having that absolute knowledge that says, 'I'm in charge here' is awfully hard for a lot of people," Laurel said. "It's especially hard for those who have been raised in the belief system that says there are aggressive forces outside ourselves that are more powerful than we are.

"I do not allow anyone, any other human, to say: 'Here's what God wants you to do,' regardless of whether it's a minister from the pulpit or a counselor or whatever. I am the one who says: 'I feel by the light of the God within me. I feel this is the thing to do. This is the decision I make.' And if I make a wrong decision, I know very well that God will not reject me for it—because sometimes my human self, the lower self, screws up. We all make mistakes, but we should take responsibility for it."

Then Laurel said the thing that made me sit down and write this book:

"I was impressed with your desire to write about this and help other people in this situation, because a lot of the kids in the psych ward are there because of attachments, spirits, possession. You could be an enormous comfort to other parents."

Chapter 9
Post Exorcism/Release

After the exorcism, channeling became a way of life for Brittany. The first week or so afterward, she channeled five or six times a day. For several days I'd wake her up in the morning to discover she displayed the characteristics of and sounded like someone else. Often the new entity seemed disoriented and confused as to where they were or why they had come to that place. After realizing Brittany had awoken as someone else, I would comfort her and hold the entity. They were usually terrified to be in a place they were totally unfamiliar with. Basing my approach on ways I had seen Laurel react to the disembodied entities possessing my daughter, I would assure the new arrival that I loved it. I would ask who it was, and sometimes engage in brief conversations. After a few minutes, it would leave and Britt would return and go downstairs to eat breakfast.

One never knew when these channeling incidents would occur. There was usually little or no warning. She'd be having a conversation with you, maybe get a bit glassy-eyed for a brief moment, and then roll her head to one side as if she were passing out. Then bam, she was someone else. I always hoped and prayed that she'd be sitting down whenever the channeling would begin, because if she was standing when the trance state took over, down she'd go. If I wasn't standing right next to her, she'd invariably slump down, plopping to the ground. Mima wasn't strong enough to hold her up, so during that period I really felt like I had to be with Brittany at all times.

The intensive channeling lasted for about two months. It happened in every room of the house and on a number of occasions when we were in the car. It almost never occurred while out in public—with the exception of Mima's birthday party at a restaurant, which I'll get to later.

I was very grateful during this time that I was able to stay at home with Brittany. Her mother had to work full time, so there was no way Britt could have stayed at her mother's house while these channeling episodes were going on.

The medical professionals at the juvenile psych ward we'd dealt with said that some of the tests they ran on Brittany indicated she apparently had long-standing and deep-seated emotional conflicts with her mother, and she had expressed a desire to return home with me. We'd been through her turning her back on one parent in favor of the other before, and we'd go through it again.

Britt's and Sheila's emotional conflicts were probably no worse than in many mother-daughter relationships. But after Britt's experiences of possession, her trauma of being in a juvenile psych ward, and to keep things as peaceful as possible—we decided it would be best if she stayed with me full time, at least for a while. Understandably, Sheila was quite upset by this turn of events, but nevertheless Brittany moved in my house on a permanent basis for about six months.

She also began counseling with Agape, a Christian-oriented counseling service group, once a week. I felt like Brittany needed a counselor experienced in parapsychology but was unable to find a parapsychologist in our area. The nearest center for the study of parapsychology was in Lexington, Kentucky, several hundred miles away—much too far to commute on a regular basis. And the hospital tests seemed to indicate that long-term therapy was in order.

The hospital counselors saw therapy as a means of helping Brittany deal with her conflicts with her mother. But her psychiatrist saw these sessions as ways to help her overcome her predisposition for "having hallucinations." Hallucinations were, of course, the official explanations for the ghosts, spirits, and demons Brittany had seen all her life and still saw on a regular basis.

I did know of a therapist in Nashville whom I had used a few times back in 1996 for job counseling. I picked Dr. Warren because I had seen an advertisement he'd run in a local magazine, in which he expressed an interest and belief in the metaphysical world. I only saw Dr. Warren for three or four sessions but came to highly respect his abilities as a therapist. And I knew from my own encounter with him that he would not dismiss Brittany's God-given talents as hallucinations and would be open-minded to her recent possession and the subsequent channeling.

But after much wrangling with the insurance company, we learned they were just not going to cover sessions with Dr. Warren. The Agape agency was the only group they'd cover. I didn't think using Agape was necessarily a bad thing, but I didn't expect them to be of much help counseling Brittany with her psychic abilities in the channeling realm.

Nevertheless, I hoped they could help her iron out her differences with her mother. That had to be a good thing and should hasten a return to some normalcy in all our lives.

Brittany was also not attending school at this time. While in the hospital, she had been taught in the unit's school, and for a week after coming home, she was still expected to attend this school. Sheila would come by and pick Britt up to take her to the hospital's juvenile psych ward in downtown Nashville every day on her way to work. Then she'd bring her home every evening.

After the sessions in the hospital, we didn't think it wise to throw her back into her previous environment at the Nashville School of the Arts, which may have contributed to her emotional instability in the first place. The breakup with her boyfriend may have actually triggered part of the emotional turmoil causing her receptivity to paranormal influences. The psychiatrist agreed, but his take on it was that the breakup might have contributed to Britt's "psychotic episodes."

So she just stayed home with me. I personally felt her emotional well-being was more important than academics at this time. We applied for home schooling status through the Metro Nashville school system.

But regardless of what was going on in our lives, the channeling continued. On average, Brittany settled into channeling mostly in the morning or from dinnertime until bedtime. She seemed to sense that I was the only one who could truly take care of her when the episodes would happen, so she followed me around the house like a puppy. She was still quite shaken and frankly scared by the events of the previous few weeks.

She didn't like being alone in the house—in fact, leaving her alone anywhere just wasn't an option. She also started leaving her bedroom door open while she slept at night.

Channeling Examples

For two months, Brittany and I were practically inseparable. If I had to go to the newspaper, to the bank, or any other errand, she came along. On many of these trips, she'd channel while we were in the car. Caring for her during this time was a full-time job.

We never knew when she was going to lose her grip on this reality, let someone else in, and start channeling. My mother simply couldn't handle the drastic changes in Britt's personality. Mima was more than willing to be there and help in any way she could—cooking, cleaning, or conversation. But I didn't feel I could leave her alone with Brittany.

Once when we were at home, Brittany channeled a boy she described as a "druggie"—a not very pleasant fellow who used street slang that was not part of Britt's vocabulary. He also said he could play the guitar, but when he picked up a guitar I'd gotten for the kids to learn on, he couldn't seem to manage it, saying: "What's up with her fingers?"—referring to his inability to manipulate Britt's hands into playing. She couldn't play, so perhaps his spirit could only manipulate the knowledge and abilities of the host. And maybe the druggie boy wasn't a separate entity at all. He talked about how he died as the result of a "bad trip" he'd been taking with his girlfriend, whom he didn't think was dead yet.

But he wasn't sure, because he said he was being kept in a dark, cold place where he couldn't see anything. And "they" only talked to him occasionally. He also stated that he hated cats, and when our cat Spot came up to him, he shouted and tried to scare it—something Brittany wouldn't do. She loves cats. He said he'd lived a bad life and wasn't proud of the things he'd done. I asked if he'd learned anything and wanted to correct his mistakes. He replied that no, he didn't plan to make any major changes. Then he said, "They're calling me. I have to go." At the time of his departure, we were sitting on the stairs. Britt slumped over and seemed unconscious for several seconds. Then she came back.

One evening as Mima was finishing dinner and Britt was sitting at the table, she channeled a young German Jewish girl who died in a concentration camp. She only spoke German, so I couldn't understand her. Britt had just taken a year and a half of German in high school, but she really wasn't by any measure proficient. I wish I had recorded the encounter, but sadly I did not. The girl was speaking in complete sentences without hesitation. I don't speak German myself, but it sounded authentic to my theatrically trained ear. Who knows? It could have been gibberish with German dialectic touches. But I'd never heard Brittany do a German accent before.

I truly wish now that I'd approached my observations of Brittany's channeling more scientifically. Video equipment at the time was quite expensive, so I didn't have any. I did have a tape recorder, and I should have recorded things—but there was never time for preparation. The channeling sessions happened out of the blue, so unless I'd been set up to record in every room, twenty-four hours a day, at less than a moment's notice, it really would have been out of the question.

I was much more concerned with making sure Brittany was physically and emotionally safe than whether anything got recorded for posterity.

But back to our little German guest: Unlike most of the entities who'd appeared at that point, this girl wouldn't let me hug her or even get very close. A quick hug always seemed to comfort the other entities who would pop in—even the druggie. But the German girl seemed afraid of me. So in order to communicate better, I gave her a pen and paper. She drew several swastikas, and a series of numbers. When I quizzically pointed to the numbers, she pointed to her wrist—supposedly indicating that these numbers were right there. I finally deduced that she meant this was the prison number the Nazis had branded on her wrist. She then stood up and started marching in time, saying "loft, writ" over and over again. Now it might seem obvious this was German for "left, right" but I didn't catch on at the time. She drew more pictures of swastikas and what looked like barbed wire, looked at me as though to say she had explained everything, then slumped over in her chair—and Britt returned. She explained to me that she could feel what the girl was feeling and could remember things from the girl's perspective. She said her father had been killed in a temple bombing, and her mother had died in a concentration camp. She had met the same fate.

The Fire Demon

Aside from the rather numerous incidents of channeling in the first two months after Britt got home from the hospital, there were four incidents in which demons tried to return. The first was the fire demon.

One morning Britt sat at the kitchen table with her grand-mother while I was running errands. Britt had a candle lit and was passing her hand across the flame. She has always been fascinated with candles and, by association, fire. Or maybe it's the other way around. Anyway, my mother told me later it looked to her like Britt was intentionally burning her wrist by heating a bobby pin over the flame and then holding the searing pin to her wrist. As soon as she noticed Mima had seen her, she quickly removed the bobby pin from her wrist, hid it and pretended nothing had happened. After I returned, Mima told me about the incident. Without appearing obvious, I later took a look at Britt's wrist. There was a burned or cut place on her wrist about an inch long running parallel to her arm. When I asked her about it, she claimed she didn't know where the mark came from. As a result, I hid the cigarette lighter she had been keeping up in her room. The next time she wanted to light a candle, she couldn't find the lighter and asked me about it. I told her I'd hid it for her own protection. She didn't argue and actually seemed to understand. So every time she wanted to light one of her candles during the next few days, she'd come to me and ask for the lighter. I'd go to my hiding place, bring it to her, and watch her while she lit the candle. Then I'd take the lighter and hide it again.

A few nights later, Britt and I were in the kitchen. It was almost bedtime. We were joking and kidding around as we often did. I finally said, "It's bedtime," and started walking toward the door to the living room.

She looked up at me, and out of the blue asked, "Where's my lighter?"

I replied that she knew where it was and knew why. I said this lightly and thought maybe she was going to make a joke out of this. Then I said, "You know, actually it's my lighter. I bought it."

Then she got that devilish expression on her face I'd seen during all the demon busting. She said, "No, actually it's my lighter, and I want it back." She sailed past me, rushing through the living room and toward the stairs. I asked where she was going, and she said she was going upstairs to find it. I told her to come back, and she replied: "You can't stop me."

The tone in her voice told me this was not Brittany talking to me. I grabbed her wrist and turned her back to me. The face that looked into my eyes was the face of a demon. She tilted her head considerably too far to one side and gave me an evil grin.

"I'm going to burn her," she hissed. She pulled away from me and rushed away, but I caught up and stopped her at the base of the stairs. I held her by the wrists to keep her from striking herself or me.

My heart was pounding and my voice quivered, but I wasn't going to let this thing have my daughter. "You're not doing this," I stammered, "not again."

"I'll do whatever I want to," it replied. "And you're scared. I can feel it."

"Maybe so, but not too scared to stop you." We struggled, and then she broke away and darted back into the kitchen. She was frantically looking for the lighter. This time I grabbed her by the shoulders and pulled her down to the floor. I'd learned at Laurel's exorcism that if you have to hold a demon down, the best technique is to pin them to the floor if you can. By now, my mother had heard the ruckus. She came in and was helping me hold Brittany's legs down. After about five minutes of this, I heard the Irish accent of Spence telling me he had everything under control and to get up off him. Now channeling Spence, I could see Brittany was out of immediate danger.

Spence, through Brittany, proceeded to tell me that we were now dealing with a fire demon—a being composed of and attracted to fire. He said he was fighting it off, and then that "its own god" totally obliterated it—because fire demons are strictly forbidden to harm human beings as it had Brittany.

As was usually his way, Spence felt inclined to linger and socialize. He mostly wanted to talk about Brittany and her progress. She had been begging me for a hamster for some reason, so he kept prodding me to go ahead and buy it for her. He usually tried to include Mima in these little discourses, and she was always a good sport and tried to be pleasant—though I'm not sure if she believed in the concept of Spence as a channeled guardian angel for Brittany or simply that this was actually just Brittany pretending (in her weakened state) to be Spence.

Finally I told Spence that we all needed to get to bed and asked if Brittany could return. He replied that she was too weak to climb the stairs, so he'd make the walk for her and let her assume her body once upstairs. So off he bounded up the stairs, showing a good deal more energy and speed than Brittany normally would have.

Spence climbed into bed for Britt and lay back telling me that she'd return soon to tell me goodnight. She seemed to pass out, and then returned to herself within a few seconds.

"Hi, Daddy, how'd I get here? What happened?" she asked innocently.

I filled my daughter in on the entire incident with the fire demon and then of Spence's subsequent nocturnal visit. But after another fifteen minutes or so, she became very sleepy and dozed off.

A Blind Date Gone Bad

Since her hospital stay, Brittany had been in close phone communication with a friend she made in the psych ward, a girl named Jeane. She lived on the other side of town. I had allowed Jeane to spend the night with us, because I thought it would be good for Brittany to have friends at this traumatic time in her life—even though it was hospital policy for former patients not to contact each other after leaving the facility. Britt and Jeane had been planning a double date to the movies. Jeane had a steady boyfriend, and she had promised Brittany she would set her up with a date too. Britt was very excited about the prospects of having a date. It would be her first real date since she and Chase broke up in October.

Jeane and Britt were bosom buddies for a while. They even talked about going off to New York together and "doing art" when they were old enough. Brittany had been very excited about this movie date for days. But the night before the date, Britt's date fell through. Jeane told her over the phone, and after Britt got off the phone she was despondent.

I tried to cheer her up and told her how she didn't need a boyfriend to validate herself. I used my own example of how I'd been single for eight years and felt that I'd gotten to know myself a lot better, and now I felt I didn't have to have someone else to be complete. She listened, but I didn't feel like she was really in agreement and still seemed very depressed.

Then suddenly she began having convulsions and shaking uncontrollably—as if she were having a seizure. After all we'd been through, this was something new. I'd been so accustomed to foreign personalities taking over Britt's body, I held her down, thinking something of that sort was about to happen. A demon or something started coming through, but after only a few moments of the old familiar hissing and growling, Spence came through and seemed to get everything under control. But just when everything seemed back to normal, the demon came out again and the convulsions resumed. Suddenly Spence came out and said, "Call Laurel. Call Laurel. I can't hold this one down." I called Laurel and luckily she was home.

Here's a transcript of the recording Laurel made later explaining what had happened to Brittany that night:

"When she feels low self-esteem, she's more of an easy mark for an entity who would like to take over," Laurel said. "That's true of virtually anybody. It loosens her sense of self-control, her sense of 'I'm in charge here.' When there's a window open for an entity to enter or a certain vulnerability for that—it's also a way for Brittany to allow some of her anger, frustration, disappointment, tumultuous emotions, etc., to be released, without taking responsibility for them. It allows her to feel, 'This is happening *to* me' as opposed to, 'It's my emotions out of control.' It's a distancing mechanism that allows her to separate herself from her own negative feelings, desires, and emotions. One of the things she needs is an acceptable way to express her emotions, including her anger—rather than letting another entity come in and be assertive.

"She draws in negative entities who are in the neighborhood. Maybe they're not full-fledged demons. They may just be floating around up there. This is a vulnerability. It's really hard for her to own her own anger, to say: 'I earned it, by God. It's mine.' She may need lessons in expressing her own anger. She may need to be encouraged to shout and scream and fling her arms—talk about her anger and get it out, because she needs a way to get it out other than turning to a surrogate."

McCartney Meets Spence

McCartney's first experience with Spence came soon after Brittany returned from the hospital. Britt, Mac, and I were talking about plans for the day, and suddenly Britt's head flopped to the side. As she looked up, we heard Spence's Irish brogue. I had cautioned Mac this might happen, so he was ready. I introduced Spence as a fallen angel, but he corrected me with: "I've amended me evil ways."

Mac proceeded to ask him questions, and treated Brittany as Spence like a major celebrity.

Spence, though, didn't seem to be that fond of children, and gave me a sideways look as if to say, "Why doesn't this kid just shut up?" But Mac was full of questions.

"Is there a heaven?" Mac asked.

"Not really," Spence answered with irritation.

"Is there a hell?" Mac asked.

"Absolutely not," Spence replied forcefully.

"Have I ever been an angel?" Mac innocently asked.

"No, no, no, that's not the way it works," Spence said with an edge.

There were lots of other questions that would only interest an eight-year-old, and Spence was rapidly growing weary of this game. Abruptly, he bid us adieu as Brittany returned.

Britt and the "Haunted House"

The next afternoon, after we'd gone to church, Brittany wanted to drive the car. She'd be turning sixteen pretty soon, so I was letting her practice driving. I was a bit concerned about her possibly falling into one of her trances, though. I expressed my concern to Spence upon one of his visits. But he said not to worry—when driving, Britt was so keenly focused on the physical reality of driving she wouldn't slip into channeling. He also said it was actually good for her at this crazy time in her life in that it forced her to stay focused on this physical reality.

So, we drove around in a subdivision behind the middle school she'd attended. Everything was going fine until we approached this one house, a split-level in a nice middle-class neighborhood. The house was probably only twenty years old or so, but it had a history. About a year earlier, the man who lived there had gone berserk and murdered his family then killed himself. Because of all the news coverage, Brittany was very familiar with the bizarre murders and the history of the house.

As we drove past the "murder house," she just stopped the car dead still in front of it.

"Brittany, what's the matter?" I asked. "Now come on, we can't just sit here in the middle of the road." She ignored me and stared blankly at the house. I shook her a little. "Britt, come on now. Just drive the car." McCartney, of course, wanted to know what was wrong with his sister. I just told him to keep quiet—that everything would be fine.

"They're still in there," she said. I was starting to become concerned that she might want to leave the car in the street and walk up to the house. Probably, I thought, the disturbed spirits associated with the house recognized that they could communicate with someone on Brittany's frequency and were calling to her. That couldn't be a good thing.

I firmly took her by the shoulders and turned her toward me. "We have to drive on," I said. "There's nothing in that house we need to associate with. Tell them you're not interested in talking with them."

She pretty much ignored me and looked back to the house.

"If you're not going to drive us out of here, I will. You decide," I said.

"Leave me alone!" she said.

It was a rather violent suggestion, which I'm not sure was directed at me or at the entities in the house. But a second later she did come to her senses enough to drive the car past the house. By now, I really thought it'd be better if she let me drive. She suddenly seemed to have gotten more reckless and less cautious. However, she still insisted on driving the car.

"Okay, we'll drive around the subdivision one more time, but then we really need to drive home." She agreed, but then we came to the intersection that would lead us back to the apparently haunted house. She got that glazed look again and seemed to automatically want to head the car off in that direction; however, I put my hand on her shoulder.

"Brittany, don't turn that way," I said. "Let's go left."

"I'm alright," she assured me.

"Well maybe so, but let's go left anyway." So she turned away from the house and we returned home without further incident.

Spence Crashes the Birthday Party

About a week after Brittany got out of the hospital, we went to a restaurant one Sunday afternoon to celebrate Mima's eightieth birthday. I was driving, Mac and Mima were in the backseat, and Britt was in the passenger seat. We stopped at a traffic light and Britt's head fell over to one side. Then Spence announced himself. Okay, Spence I could handle, but demons weren't invited to the party.

He asked us where we were going, and when I told him, he wished Mima a happy birthday. Mima chatted just a bit with Spence, but she never seemed to know just quite how to take him. She probably felt Spence was just some kind of projection of Brittany's emotional state. She would sometimes talk to Spence as if she were still talking to Brittany, e.g., telling Spence/Brittany: "I love you." Then Spence would shake his head and reply, "Well, isn't that nice?" and look at her like *she* was the crazy one. So we rode along, with Mima humoring Brittany/Spence, McCartney asking him a million questions about the true nature of the cosmos as seen through the eyes of an eight-year-old, and I mostly just hoping he'd let Britt come back out soon.

But he didn't. We arrived at the restaurant, and Spence was still having a grand old time. I then asked Spence point-blank if he didn't think he should let Brittany come back for our birthday luncheon.

"Oh, no! I asked her," he replied, "and she said it'd be fine for me to stay. Don't worry, Bill. Everything's grand."

We were seated and began examining the menu. I had to explain much of it to Spence as he didn't seem to understand what the names of American dishes represented. He finally settled on fish and chips, a dish Brittany didn't like. So here we were, this little family—father, son, grandma, and who else? The waitress seemed more than a little puzzled by Spence/Brittany's Irish accent and often had to ask for clarification. This seemed to irritate Spence considerably. I just smiled, nodded toward Spence, and said, "Foreign student."

The food was late, and Spence had several cryptic remarks for the waitress concerning punctuality. Then he didn't like his fish: "Not yet cooked then, is it?" He demanded it be sent back till it was to his liking. Brittany wouldn't have done that in a million years, but Spence loudly decreed that he get first class service.

All in all, though, Spence was humorous and fun to be with, and the birthday celebration was quite pleasurable—but also quite strange. Definitely the oddest birthday bash Mima ever had.

McCartney wanted to stop by the restroom on the way out.

"I'll take him," Spence volunteered and started marching toward the men's room with Mac.

"You can't go in there," I said just in time. "You have to go in that one," pointing to the ladies' room.

"Oh yes, sorry. Well, this'll be odd, won't it?" he said as he went into the women's restroom.

Finally back at home, I asked Spence if he didn't think he should let Brittany return so we could open Mima's presents. He reluctantly agreed, but like a proper Irish gentleman, thanked us for having him over. Then I held Britt's head as she changed gears.

When she learned she'd missed lunch she was more than a little upset.

"Oh, man! Why does he do that?"

"He told us you said it was okay," I said.

"Yeah, just to pop in and say hello—not to eat my lunch!" She didn't remember what anything tasted like. Just as well, since it was fish.

The Aphrodite Episode

One of our more interesting channeling incidents was the time Brittany channeled the ancient Greek goddess Aphrodite. This might be an example of channeling an entity to express her fears rather than feeling them too deeply.

Brittany was still very depressed about not having a boyfriend. Since she was being kept home from school since her stay in the hospital a few weeks earlier, she wasn't in contact with kids her own age. She still felt pretty isolated.

As we sat together on the sofa one day, making small talk, we discussed the possibility of when and where she might return to school, when her friend Jeane might come over, and other mundane issues. Then she got that glazed, starry look in her eyes. Her head lolled over to one side, and she passed out for a moment. When she came to, she had a frightened look. She then physically pulled away from me on the couch as if she were afraid of me. By now, I knew the drill.

I told her not to be afraid, that I loved her, and I wanted to help. She still seemed more than a bit apprehensive. I asked who she was.

"Aphrodite," she said in a tiny little voice much smaller than Brittany's own.

"As in the Greek goddess Aphrodite?" I asked, a bit incredulous.

"Yes."

I told her that this was indeed an honor and was curious as to why she'd come to visit.

"I'm worried about her," she said.

Things were going so much better than they had been a few weeks earlier, I told my new visitor there was nothing to worry about. Everything seemed to be under control for a change.

"No, it's not. Unless some important changes are made, she won't be here past the age of seventeen."

I asked Aphrodite if this gloomy forecast could be averted. She said yes, but she didn't know how. She was very evasive about just what changes needed to be made to ensure that Brittany would not meet with such a premature demise, but she was adamant about me seeing to Britt's welfare or bad things could be expected. As I did all the other entities Britt channeled, I tried to hug her to show a degree of compassion. The great majority of them responded positively to this; however, Aphrodite would have none of it. She pulled away and simply said, "Take care of her. I have to go." Britt slumped over for a few seconds then came back as herself. And that was the end of my encounter with a Greek goddess.

As I look back over everything that has happened over the last eighteen years, I can see that there was a great deal of merit in what Aphrodite was predicting. At the time, I thought the worst of it was over and that we were out of the woods. The goddess was inaccurate in predicting that Britt wouldn't make it past seventeen, but she was correct in foreseeing that there would be abundant perils ahead.

Chapter 10
The Hitchhiking Demon

Around the middle of February 2001, I took Brittany and Mc-Cartney to see a play. The kids and I were walking back to the car from the show. Britt and McCartney got into an argument, and she was really being more than a bit hard on him. I pointed that out to her. Then she and I got into an argument, with her saying "you always take his side." In fact, I was much more likely to be calling him down. Although he's grown up to be a Navy vet, graduating from Northern Arizona University, he was a very rambunctious youngster and a bit prone to getting into trouble. Britt and I argued extensively in the car on the way to take Mac home.

First, we had to travel to Britt's friend Jeane's home to return some clothes Jeane had left at our house. This is the neighborhood where Brittany's ex-boyfriend lived, and she had told me before that she didn't want to drive through it, saying it stirred up too many old memories. I understood this and took a much longer route to get to and from Jeane's house.

However, this time I accidentally got very near Chase's house. It was dark, and I missed my street and got a bit lost. Brittany absolutely freaked out when she realized where we were. She started screaming and crying and accusing me of bringing her there on purpose. This upset me, because it was a total accident—so I started yelling back. The atmosphere in the car got pretty tense for several minutes. Poor McCartney just sat quietly in the backseat, hoping not to get caught in the crossfire.

Eventually we arrived at Jeane's house and dropped off the clothes; however, Britt and I were still arguing. Finally, things became more peaceful and we just sat in silence till we arrived at McCartney's mother's home. Nothing had been resolved—we just called a truce. We dropped Mac off and began the trip back to our house, about a forty-minute journey.

Before we were even out of Mac's subdivision, Britt allowed Spence to take over. He began by telling me he was "not here to be friends" and admonished me for reprimanding Brittany, blaming me for the whole argument.

Later I told Laurel about this incident, because it would eventually involve a demonic presence. Her taped comments follow:

"This is an example of where Spence is playing the alter ego role and negotiating," Laurel said. "Brittany doesn't feel strong enough to negotiate this for herself. Believe me, Spence was better than some of the other alternatives."

I replied to Spence that Brittany was my daughter and I couldn't allow her to talk to me in the manner she'd used. I admitted that perhaps I'd been a bit harsh on her, but she had to learn that she simply had to show me a bit of respect and refrain from launching into these verbal tirades.

Then Spence replied that, "It wasn't her. It was a demon trying to come through."

Then it began saying things like, "I'm going to take her soul where you'll never find her." Punctuated with growling and hysterical laughter, this was a pretty terrifying situation. Then somewhere along the way, it started singing "Jesus Loves Me" again. So I'm singing "Joy to the World"; it's singing "Jesus Loves Me"; and we're both getting louder and louder. Finally my stronger voice drowned it out, and it gave that up. It decided instead to argue with me, telling me how it had "come to get Brittany."

Then I remembered things I'd heard Laurel say about how this whole demon thing had simply been like a play, a game to the dark angels. I began repeating the things I'd heard Laurel telling the demons on the night of the release/exorcism: "You've done a good job. You've acted your part well. God appreciates your good work. No one's going to punish you. No one's going to send you to hell. You won't burn forever and ever. God wants you to return to him, and it's time to return. It's time for you to return to God and be rewarded."

This went on for twenty minutes or so. I was essentially giving a sermon to the demon. Using Spence as a reference, I mentioned him, saying: "Spence is angry with me right now, but I love him anyway. He was a dark angel like you at one time. He saw the light, and this kind of transformation will work for you. I'm trying to help you here, and I want you to be smart enough to accept this help. Spence was smart enough to see the advantages of accepting this help, and I'm sure you're as smart a man as Spence is."

Then it said, "I'm not a man; I'm a girl."

So I just replied: "Okay then, I'm sure you're just as smart a lady."

Eventually, I must have gotten to it on some level. It started crying and didn't say anything. It just cried. That went on for a few minutes, and then Britt slumped over onto my shoulder. After a moment, she came up and was Brittany again. Of course, she was still mad at me. She turned toward the window and wouldn't even look at me.

Finally we arrived home. It had been a grueling ordeal. I told Brittany how much I loved her. Curiously, she replied: "I didn't think you did." I finally convinced her everything was okay with us and we went upstairs after she told Mima hello.

I have had a number of encounters with the paranormal since first being introduced to the Patience Worth entity back in the seventies. However, I'd have to say that my ride on a lonely road with the hitchhiking demon has to rank at the top of the list for pure fear factor.

Isabella

After we got upstairs, Britt began playing with her hamster (which I had bought for her just a week earlier, partially at Spence's insistence). Then she put the hamster (which she'd named Angel Mouse) back in its cage, sat on the bed, fell into a trance, and came out channeling a little girl named Isabella who said she'd died in 1895. It turned out that Isabella was the little girl in the yellow dress that had been released the night of the exorcism. Even though her spirit had been released, she had been with Brittany for a long time and Britt had the ability to call Isabella back, whom it turns out had a bit of a dark side.

Isabella's visit was somewhat of a relief after my encounter that night with the hitchhiking demon. She wanted to play with the hamster, saying she had had one in her lifetime. Then she walked all about the upstairs, exploring, and marveling at the electrical gadgets. She played with the light switch and said they had electric lights in her day, but they weren't very reliable. I finally had to ask her not to fiddle with the lights, or mine wouldn't be much more reliable than the ones she was used to. She then went into the bathroom and gazed at herself in the mirror (like most teenagers do).

"She's not very pretty," she said, referring to Brittany.

"Well, I think she is."

"You would. You're her father. I killed *my* father," she said matter-of-factly. "I murdered both my parents."

I didn't ask how. This really wasn't a road I wanted to go down. I was also taken aback just a bit by her lack of remorse. But I plunged on with:

"You know they would forgive you now," I told Isabella. "All that's behind you. Maybe you were possessed by some kind of demon like Brittany." I repeated that I was sure her parents had forgiven her.

"Oh yes, I know," she said nonchalantly. "We ironed all that out."

Standing in the upstairs bathroom, she decided to play with the light switch again. I told her it was getting pretty late and maybe she should let Brittany come back so she could go to bed. She was very reluctant to leave, but finally gave in. I hugged her and kissed her on the cheek. Brittany came back very tired and eager to go to bed and call it a day.

This had been a very strange little evening.

Laurel's perspective was that Brittany needed to get to the bottom of using surrogates to express her fears, anger, uncertainties, and frustrations. She suggested I explain to Britt that I still loved her even if she'd done something wrong and I had to correct her. She said there was "an awful lot of anger there that's genuinely Brittany's." She was using these surrogates to process it. She said Britt needed to be able to express herself, even including saying things I'd otherwise find unacceptable. Laurel suggested that though the entities were genuine, Brittany wasn't always as out of it as she and the entity might lead me to believe—at least on her subconscious level.

The Supposed "Good" Demon

Since Brittany was staying at my house after she came home from the hospital, she asked Sheila to let her come by her place and pick up some of her things. Sheila put us off for several weeks, un-happy, I suppose that the hospital had claimed she and Britt had is-sues they needed to work out. She even had the locks changed on her house, so we couldn't get in during the day and get the things Brittany wanted.

Finally, the counselor at Agape told Sheila she was making things worse by not letting Brittany have her things. So we went to Sheila's one night and picked up a carload of stuff. Sheila was extremely pleasant, showing Britt the new puppies her dog had had and talking a long time. Britt and I were also quite civil, and I thought everything had gone very well.

We got back to my house and brought in the stash of goodies. Mima was sitting on the sofa. Brittany said: "That was the acting job of my life. I am just exhausted"—insinuating that her friendli-ness to her mother was all an act. I had asked Britt to help me put some of her things up, but now it seemed that she was just too tired from her Oscar-winning performance.

"Well, I'm exhausted too," I replied, "but we've got to get this stuff put up." She bristled at my lack of concern as to the degree of her fatigue. So then she appeared to want to get into an argument about who was the most tired.

So as a seeming reaction to me telling her that she was no more exhausted than I, Brittany went into convulsions—shaking all over uncontrollably, eyes rolled back and head lulled over. Then she fell into the floor. I rushed to her, thinking one of the demons was coming back.

She began growling and hissing, so I go into my newly acquired minister mode and repeated the Unity benediction: "May the spirit of God surround us; may the love of God enfold us; may the power of God protect us; may the presence of God watch over us; wherever we are God is, and all is well." I repeated this over and over, sometimes substituting "us" with "you," so as to direct my chant more toward the demon.

The demon began speaking in some indecipherable language and looking at me like I was supposed to be able to respond to this. Naturally, I had no idea what it was saying.

After much wrangling, eventually Spence came through and said: "Get off of me, you big lummox." He paused as I got up. "I just want you to know I'm still mad at you. And you also made a mistake here. That was a good demon, not a bad one."

I asked how that could be. I'd never heard of a good demon; however, he pretty much ignored that particular entreaty. Then I said that it seemed to want to communicate, but I couldn't understand the language it was speaking in.

"You need to learn more languages," he responded.

So I'm thinking, *How am I supposed to learn Demon Talk?* I saw that as a very unrealistic suggestion.

I asked Laurel about the existence of so-called good demons.

"By definition, we don't use the term demon to refer to someone who is good," Laurel replied in a taped conversation. "So if this happens again, you might ask Spence, 'Are you saying that it's a good entity?' And encourage him to take a neutral tone. Then talk about what makes this a good entity, and what message does this one seek to bring? If there's helpfulness in it, certainly you want to hear it.

"Remember that powerful entities can seem scary simply because of the power factor. This may have been a powerful but not negative entity trying to speak as a new voice through her. Sometimes when a new voice comes through, it takes them a while to get the drill. Voices have come through me making sounds I wouldn't have thought my throat could make."

"It was hissing like a cat," I said. "I told Spence this and asked him how I was supposed to react to something hissing at me."

Laurel told me this episode might have arisen because I have "a strong reincarnational connection to the cat god, Baast," and it may have been trying to communicate.

"You have an energy and a collection of past life experiences that is strong without being aggressive," Laurel said. "This may have been a cat trying to come through and speak to you. If this happens again, just say, 'In our language, hissing is considered a symbol of conflict. Is that what you mean? If that's what you mean, let's find a way to mutually communicate and express this.'"

Blood on the Floor

The last example of out-and-out demonic activity being channeled through Brittany during this early period happened one Sunday evening while I was sitting at the computer writing my weekly theatre review for the newspaper. Brittany was sitting on the floor watching television, and Mima was sitting on the sofa working one of her crossword puzzles.

I would write my reviews and then email them to the newspaper. I finished this one up and put it (I thought) in the "Mail Waiting to be Sent" file. Then I got up to do something else, came back, and got positioned to call the review up and send it off. But it was nowhere to be found. It hadn't been saved. I freaked out! These reviews usually take about three hours to write, so I could see all that hard work going down the drain. I don't remember exactly what I said, but I'm sure there were a few profane expletives. I got up, did a bit of pacing, and tried to decide what to do. I hadn't made a hard copy of the review, so it was just *gone*. I didn't know how I could have been so stupid.

I was very angry with myself, but Brittany is such a hypersensitive person she seemed to perceive my anger as being directed at her. So I went into the kitchen to do a bit more yelling at myself. I rarely get mad, but when I do—my wailing and gnashing of teeth can be regretfully excessive. And, of course, it was obvious to Mima and Britt that I was going overboard.

As is true with most kids, Brittany knows a lot more about computers than I do. I felt like the review was perhaps in there somewhere, I just didn't know how to find it. I asked her if she'd take a look and see if she could find it and was more than a bit dismayed by her lack of concern.

Brittany said to "calm down" and that she'd find it. I stopped baying at the moon and thanked her for her help.

But sure enough, she was no more successful than I was at finding it. I announced I'd "rewrite it tomorrow" and turned the computer off. Brittany got up and went into the kitchen.

As I got up from the computer, she came into the living room and sat on the arm of an easy chair. She had that glassy look on her face—the look I had come to dread. I told her I was sorry I had yelled and hugged her. She still had this glazed look. I asked if everything was alright.

"I'm not going to clean it up," she said.

"Clean what up?" I asked.

"Just go in the kitchen and look," she answered. "See for yourself. I'm not cleaning it up."

I had no idea what she was talking about. I just thought maybe she had spilled something in the kitchen and for some reason was refusing to clean it up. But that vacant look was bothering me more than anything else. So I went into the kitchen to see what she was talking about. I looked all around and saw nothing. I then returned to the living room where Brittany was still sitting on the arm of the chair.

"There's nothing in there. I don't know what you're talking about," I said. "I don't see anything to clean up."

"The blood," she replied. "It's all over the floor, all over the walls. I'm not cleaning it up." I became alarmed at the mention of blood and was beginning to anticipate another episode.

"Okay, come with me," I said. "Show me what you're talking about." We both returned to the kitchen.

"There, the blood. It's everywhere," she gestured. "I'm not cleaning it up." She turned to go back into the living room. I stopped her, took her arm, and turned her to face me.

"Brittany, there is no blood anywhere," I replied. "You're seeing things. You need to snap out of this." She just stared at me blankly. I was beginning to get a little scared. "Now come on back to me. You don't need to go there. Let's come back to reality."

She cocked her head to one side and gave me that evil smirk of a grin I'd seen from demons on previous occasions. "Brittany's not here," it said.

"Hello, Sally!" I exclaimed. Now I have no idea where that Sally came from. I felt like I recognized this entity, and Sally is just the first thing that flew out of my mouth. Maybe it was just a sign of my exasperation at having to go through yet another episode. Brittany began making inarticulate growling noises, and her head started rolling back and forth as if it were in danger of becoming disengaged from her shoulders. I took her firmly by the shoulders as she began falling to the floor. She began writhing and rolling in the floor in a sort of exaggerated convulsion. I shouted for Mima to come and help me restrain her. My eighty-year-old mother had come to recognize what was going on and immediately got down on the floor with us to help hold Brittany down.

The struggle was similar to others we had experienced in the last two months but of shorter duration. I went into my ritual of reciting the Unity benediction, inviting the entity to return to the light and its rightful place with God. After ten to fifteen minutes of this, Spence popped in and told us he had everything under control.

"Where did that one come from and what caused all that?" I asked. He just said he didn't know but that everything was alright now.

As was typical with Spence, he was hungry and thirsty. Claiming he'd been a baker in his life in Ireland, Spence/Brittany proceeded to make a concoction of corn flakes, melted butter, and sugar—which he hungrily wolfed down.

After Spence had satisfied his hunger, I suggested he let Brittany return since it was getting late. He volunteered to "walk her up the stairs," since she'd be pretty exhausted from our little battle with the demon. He got her dressed for bed, crawled in, and finally, Britt returned. She asked what had happened, and I explained about the entire incident. By now she had come to accept these things as just a part of life, so she smiled, kissed me goodnight and went to sleep.

The Play, Spence, and Other Changes

The channeling was just a regular part of our lives, five or six times a day, for about two months. It abruptly ended about the middle of March.

I had written a play, which my theatre company was set to produce in May. I wasn't supposed to direct the show, but as playwright and producer I'd need to be at auditions and nearly every rehearsal. So I asked Britt to be my personal assistant.

With her having all these unannounced channeling episodes, I couldn't leave her alone with my mother at night. I was more than a bit worried that Britt would have one of her spells right in the middle of rehearsals, but there was just nothing I could do about that. So she was just going to have to be there with me where I could keep an eye on her.

At first she was very enthused about helping me and seemed grateful to be able to take part in the show, looking forward to it. During our two weekends of auditions, everything went great. Brittany did a terrific job in her position of playwright's assistant and seemed to be having a really good time. I watched her closely, but she never seemed even close to a channeling bout.

Like the driving, I suppose her new position kept her too focused on the here and now to slip into other dimensions.

Then just about the time we got ready to begin rehearsals, Brittany lost interest in being my assistant. She had been despondent about not having a boyfriend, and it didn't do any good for me to tell her that liking yourself was more important than having someone else like you—or that loving yourself is a necessity if any relationship is going to work out. At times, she almost seemed obsessed with talk of finding a new boyfriend.

Then she discovered this boy, Dave, who lived in the same condo complex we did. They seemed to really hit it off and started spending lots of time together after school was out. I was happy for Britt because this seemed to make her happy.

Of course now that she had someone to keep her occupied, she wasn't so eager to go with me to rehearsals every night. She begged to be able to stay at home with her grandmother, but Mima just wouldn't go along with that. It had only been a very short time since Brittany was frequently channeling—and it hadn't been that long since we'd even been visited by the occasional demon. So like it or not, Britt was stuck with going to rehearsals with me. Her thoughts were elsewhere, though, and she abandoned my rehearsals for a friend's play that was rehearsing down the hall from us. So much for my valuable assistant.

As time wore on for the next six to eight weeks, the new boyfriend became the most important thing in her universe. And except for an occasional visit from Spence, channeling and demonic possession faded into history.

During the first few weeks of rehearsals for my show, we were driving to the theatre one evening, and Brittany got that distant look in her eyes like she was about to go into a trance. I asked her how she felt and what was going on, and she said Spence wanted to come through. But she consciously seemed to be making an effort to remain in the here and now. I commented that that was probably wise at that particular time, since we were almost at the theatre. It might be difficult to explain Spence to the cast.

I didn't hear any more from Spence until a few days after my play had closed. Then one night we were getting ready for bed. I sat on Britt's bed to kiss her goodnight when I heard that familiar Irish brogue.

"It's me you'd be kissin', so I'd just as soon you didn't," Spence said.

"Hello, my friend. Listen, it's bedtime," I replied. "Could you possibly come back tomorrow during the day when we'd have more time?"

"I'll take but a moment of your precious time," he said a bit sarcastically.

But it turned out he really didn't have anything earthshaking to say—only that we hadn't talked in a long while, and he just wanted to see how I was doing and tell me he was keeping his eyes on Brittany. He also seemed very fond of the new boyfriend, Dave, and thought this was a wonderful thing for Britt. Of course, in his position as her advocate, I'd hardly have expected him to say anything else. Then he left, promising to come back in the next few days for a more extended visit. However, I didn't hear from him again for over two months.

By early July, Britt had reconciled with her mother and had moved back in with her pretty much full time. This was a bit hard for me to handle at first, since Britt had told me she wanted to live with me full time. From mid-January till mid-April, Britt had been very antagonistic toward her mother. But then, around Easter time, things started thawing. I suppose I had become very protective of Brittany after the possession, exorcism, and subsequent channeling—and it was difficult to let her go. But I knew deep inside this was for the best. I knew she loved her mother and missed her, and I hoped they *would* be able to mend fences, because Britt needed her mother.

Also, by this time Britt and I hadn't been getting along nearly as well—essentially since about the time Dave came onto the scene. Brittany had become quite rebellious concerning all things Dave. I had always been a very lenient-type parent (probably much too much so), but I did have a few rules. These were rules that Britt chose to not follow very well. So we ended up at cross-swords for really the first major time in her life. This is probably pretty common during the transition from childhood to adolescence, but it was hard on me—especially since we had been so close during those months following the possession.

After Britt returned to live at her mother's, she also began attending church with Sheila. The congregation was a nondenominational, rather fundamentalist group—closer to the style of worship Sheila had grown up with before becoming an Episcopalian when she married me. The church was having a kind of summer revival, with a nationally recognized speaker or "prophet," as they called him, leading the nightly services. Brittany was expected to attend these with her mother. As fate would have it, Spence also heard the prophet.

Britt had spent the day with me because Sheila had to work on Saturdays, and I was supposed to take her to the church at 6:30 p.m. to meet her mom. I had been invited, but respectfully declined.

Back at my house, Brittany had gone upstairs to take a shower. I could hear her up there playing her music and singing. Time for the service was fast approaching, so I called up to hurry her along. She came down the steps with an Irish twinkle in her eye.

"Don't you be rushin' me, now."

"Spence?"

"I don't know why I'm here, but I am," he said shaking his head.

It seems Brittany had summoned him to be her surrogate at the church service. We chatted for a bit, then I said we'd better be going. Naturally, he headed for the kitchen saying he was hungry, as he always did. I had to steer him out the door or we'd be late. We arrived at the church, but Sheila wasn't there yet. So we just sat in the car and talked while we waited.

He seemed to be unaware of what had been going on in Britt's and my relationship. So I filled him in and expressed my concerns with her recent rejection of me, and her dramatic turn-around in embracing her mom. I was sincerely happy she had let her mom back into her life. She needed us both, but I found it confusing that she couldn't seem to embrace both of us at the same time.

I think I was actually more comfortable dealing with demons.

Spence seemed to have no control over his being summoned to stand in as Brittany's proxy at the revival. I asked him if he wasn't supposed to be the one in charge, since he was the angel. He didn't seem to know how to respond to that. He just knew this was something he had to do to help Brittany. Still, he was in one of his grand moods, so we sat in the car making jokes. I remember one of his witticisms concerned returning to heaven after the service to report back to Jesus about how humans were handling his message down here now.

"I don't think he'd like it much, the way they've turned his words around," he said seriously. "He has a great sense of humor, you know, but I don't think he'd find this too funny."

Finally Sheila arrived. I let Britt/Spence out, and they went into the church. I asked her later if she remembered any of the service, and she said no. I also asked if her mother ever caught on that it was Spence sitting next to her and not Brittany. She replied that Spence could "do her accent" so that no one would be the wiser.

I had seen that happen once at my house. Spence was pulling the control switches for Britt, when the phone rang. I answered, and it was one of Brittany's friends. Spence took the phone.

"I can handle it," the Irishman said. "Watch this."

So he began talking to Britt's friend in her voice and accent. He kept giving me looks like he didn't have a clue as to what the little girl on the other end was talking about, but he was very polite to her, using only very short answers and responses. He seemed to be trying to get off the phone as quickly as possible. So I suppose that's the way it went that night in church. Short answers and lots of smiles.

Werewolves at the Campsite

Britt did return to stay with me for a few nights to go on a brief camping trip with McCartney to Montgomery Bell State Park near Dickson, Tennessee.

As Brittany, McCartney, and I were erecting our tent and other campsite paraphernalia about three p.m., Britt got this panicky look on her face and dropped the box she was carrying from the car. She said she'd seen an ominous dark shadow approaching us but wouldn't really elaborate.

Britt started rushing around, making crosses and pentagrams in the dirt around out campsite. She never really explained this action, but after a few minutes everything seemed fine and we got back to the business of setting up camp and enjoying our vacation. Then that night, after returning from a bit of fishing and dinner at the park's inn/restaurant, we turned in early and called it a day.

It's common for me to awaken four to seven times during the night due to chronic insomnia. I go to the bathroom; I go back to sleep. Although I was sleeping in a sleeping bag on the ground in a tent, my nightly ritual would not be deterred.

But this night there was an unexpected twist. Every time I awakened, I'd get out of the sleeping bag, go to the camp restroom, and come back—but I thought I kept hearing a dog growling. It sounded like he was about ten feet away, following me to the restroom, then back to the tent. Then the mutt seemed to lurk outside the tent as I curled back into the sleeping bag. I could hear it rustling the leaves on the other side of the canvas wall.

But I never saw anything. Now I just assumed that one of the other campers had brought their dog, and he was wandering the campgrounds.

I was a bit unnerved by being growled at, but it didn't scare me. Dogs growl. Leave them alone, and they'll leave you alone. I didn't even think it was worth mentioning to the kids the next morning.

The next day was filled with fishing and swimming, and the kids seemed to be having a great time. We built a fire that night, cooked out, and then got ready to turn in. The campsite had been put in order, and the three of us were just about to enter the tent when Britt stopped in her tracks.

"Don't move," she said.

"What is it?" I asked. She had that panicky look on her face I'd grown all too familiar with. Mac was tense.

"There are wolves all around us. Can't you see them? Can't you hear them?" Well of course we couldn't. This was obviously one of those psychic things that Mac and I weren't privy to.

But Brittany insisted that there was a pack of wolves encircling us. They were all growling and snarling except for the leader of the pack. Brittany said the leader was a white wolf and a female. It came up to her wanting to be petted. Britt leaned over and stroked the thin air at about the height where a very large dog might have been.

"It's okay," Britt said. "She likes me. She won't let the others bother us." So not really knowing what else to do, I reached over to pet the wolf too. However, Brittany told me I was standing on her tail. Ah, well.

The next morning we found a notice tacked to the bulletin board in the washhouse saying there would be a film and lecture in the park that week about the legend of "werewolves" in Montgomery Bell State Park. None of us had ever heard about such a legend before.

We all jumped into the car and rushed down to the park office to find out about the werewolf legend. The lady at the information desk seemed to know very little about it, and the person who did was on vacation. However, if we'd just attend the film on Thursday evening, we'd learn all about it. Naturally we had to leave on Tuesday to get Britt back to her summer job. However, Mac and I drove all the way back to Montgomery Bell that Thursday night to learn about the werewolf.

Turned out "werewolf" is just a term the locals used for the creatures many people swear they've seen in the area of the park—including wealthy nineteenth-century industrialist Montgomery Bell himself. Actually, the animal appears to be more along the lines of a Sasquatch or Bigfoot. An apelike, hairy humanoid. However, unlike the sightings of the meek vegetarian Sasquatch in other areas, this version seems to be carnivorous. The pack or tribe had often attacked livestock. Many cows and sheep had disappeared. Montgomery Bell himself claimed to have witnessed a man killed by the beast.

Whether there is any connection between Brittany's ghostly pack of wolves and the area's legendary werewolf, I cannot say.

Laurel's Final Take on Britt's Situation

"I don't sense a continued demonic presence in Brittany," Laurel surmised about eight months after the exorcism. "She may be calling other entities when she needs them—times when she feels she doesn't know what to say or how to deal with things and feels some other being would do the job that she wants done better than her: such as making you afraid to argue with her.

"This is on the unconscious level, not the conscious Brittany. Now she *must* allow this on some level. They can't operate through her unless she allows it on some level, even to the extent that she might be just too afraid *not* to allow it. People can be so scared that they're sometimes afraid to claim their strength, and they just let things happen.

"I take responsibility for deciding who speaks through me," Laurel continued. "Sometimes they do just 'bop in' as they do for Brittany. But if I say, 'Everybody out!' then they all have to get out. I'm hoping Brittany will embrace that concept and use it."

Laurel volunteered to teach Britt the ins and outs of psychic management, and I was looking forward to their first lesson.

Chapter 11
It's Not Over

I had smugly thought the above paranormal/psychic events spanning January through August 2001 had concluded. In fact, I was so confident of the big bad's demise that I had begun talking to my friend Joel about developing our family's harrowing tale into a play. Hoping the calamity that had befallen us might help others faced with the same dilemma, I contemplated turning our disaster into a dramatic work from which others might benefit. Since I felt too close to the subject matter to be completely objective, I approached Joel about a collaboration.

Because we kept in touch over the phone occasionally, I had generally kept Joel appraised of our ongoing war with the demons—but he really didn't know the details. After reading the journal I'd kept, though, Joel was basically spellbound by what we'd been going through. Having known him for years and been in a play he directed, Brittany also considered Joel a close friend. She was eager to see him get involved, I wanted to get the story out there, and he was quite eager to help me develop the material into a play. We had several meetings in which we discussed possible approaches.

Brittany was living with Sheila full time, except for the week we went camping in mid-July. Other than a few phone calls a week and an occasional Saturday spent at my house, Britt and I had had very little contact until mid-October.

It was the most extensive period I'd been separated from my daughter since her birth nearly sixteen years earlier. It was very hard on me, and I was quite depressed about it for the first month or so. But Britt and I had had some pretty rough anti-bonding times during the final two months she had stayed exclusively with me. The new boyfriend, Dave, was nearly two years older than Britt, and looking back I guess I should have seen red flags go up simply because of that. I didn't discourage them getting together, because after all she had been through with the possessions and wrangling with psychiatrists and therapists, I really felt like she deserved a good time for a change.

But the closer Britt and Dave became, the more my relationship with my daughter deteriorated. I suppose it was natural that the two of them would want to spend as much time together as possible.

But Brittany and I were arguing more than we'd ever done. So, when she announced she was ready to go back to her mother's and stay for a while I wasn't really surprised.

At this point, I was the "bad guy" who made rules—rules that Brittany didn't want to keep.

I blamed myself for her alienation, but I know now I was just fulfilling my role as a parent. Brittany had never had many rules. I suppose Sheila and I had always been too lenient on her. We were in our thirties when she was born and hadn't really expected to have any children. Then we divorced when she was four, and both of us were too easy on her in a misguided attempt to win Britt's favor. As a result, Britt never really had chores like many children, and we both catered to her far more than we should have.

So it actually was quite natural for her to rebel when I finally did place rules and restrictions on her.

Britt and I probably had more arguments during the three months since Dave entered the scene than we had had during her entire existence up to that point.

I tried very hard not to let my dejection show when she chose to move in with Sheila—possibly because Sheila had already gotten the cold shoulder from Brittany for nearly five months. I didn't whine about the situation, because I was just getting a dose of what Sheila already had.

By October, though, my relations with Britt had improved quite a bit. We were spending more time together, and the arguing had almost ceased altogether. Her mom had a second job on weekends, so occasionally Britt would stay with me while Sheila worked.

Sometimes we'd go see a movie or maybe just hang around the house. Naturally Dave was still in the picture, but I tried my best just to accept him—knowing that the quickest way to turn my daughter against me would be to openly reject her choice of boyfriends.

Brittany got a part-time job as an actor in a local haunted house called Shocktober. She seemed to really love this, getting to dress up, portray various demented characters, and exercise her acting legs.

But it was about this time that Brittany told me she felt like the demons were "trying to come back." She said she could hear voices calling her name. She also said she had started seeing apparitions on a more regular basis over at her mother's house. I asked if she'd told Sheila any of this, and Britt said she "didn't want to upset her" and didn't think Sheila would believe her anyway.

With demons potentially at the proverbial door again, action had to be taken immediately. Everyone involved was emotionally frayed around the edges, and the wicks of our candles had just about totally burned out. But because we had already been tested by fire and survived the initial onslaught, I didn't feel quite as helpless as I had back in January. Under Laurel's tutelage, I had learned more about demonic possession than I had ever anticipated I would in this lifetime—and had learned more than I certainly ever really wanted to know.

Laurel Leaves the Picture

However, I couldn't depend on Laurel anymore. She said Sheila had called and told her to "stay away from my daughter." I suppose this would have been during those months when Brittany wasn't having anything to do with her mother—but I don't know for sure. I was quite upset that Laurel was refusing to help. The woman who had exorcised the original demons and freed our daughter from their grasp had been supposedly forbidden from offering any more assistance. I did my best to get Laurel to overlook this banishment, but she regretfully said she had to honor Sheila's request. She was, after all, Brittany's mother.

I had hoped Laurel would be able to work with Brittany and help her develop her gift—to help her not be afraid of the things she saw, and to learn how to manage them. Although, of course, I didn't agree—looking back, I can at least see things from Sheila's perspective now. We were all dealing with unseen forces we'd never had to handle before—and we all had to deal with them from our own spiritual vantage points. Sheila's vantage point was traditional, evangelical Christianity. Laurel herself was Christian, even if a bit of an unconventional one, and she had tried to tailor Brittany's cleansing/exorcism with as much of a Christian spiritual slant as possible *because* she thought this would help Sheila better relate. But in the end, her exorcism probably had a bit too much of a New Age slant to it for Sheila to accept.

But none of that was helping me now. Laurel had been my first line of defense against the entities trying to possess Brittany, but now that option was off the table. Laurel's help was no longer available.

I was angry at Laurel for refusing to help further and terribly, terribly confused about what to do next.

My daughter was again being assaulted by evil, unseen entities and I had to find someone to help.

I called several local metaphysically oriented people I knew just to get more than one opinion. I first rang up an old friend of mine named Marian "Daystar" Bustamonte. Daystar was her spiritual name, and that's what everyone in the Nashville metaphysical community called her. She hated being called Marian. Daystar was, in fact, my teacher for the class in Wicca. She is also a Native American shaman.

My six-week course in Wicca taught me lots about things I'd never been exposed to before, and I came to regard Daystar as a good friend and trusted spiritual adviser. Although I finally returned to my own form of Christian faith, I developed the greatest respect for Pagans and those who utilize this belief system in a sincere attempt to access the available power of God to accomplish good in the world.

I hadn't burdened Daystar with the nightmare we'd been through nor told her about Brittany's possession when it happened. There was just too much going on for me to wrap my head around everything I should do and everyone I should tell. But on that October morning, I called Daystar to see if she could offer any advice. By this point, I was desperate and didn't much care about offending anyone's religious sensibilities. My daughter was begging me for help, and I went to the best source I knew of.

Her roommate answered and told me Daystar had moved to North Carolina and gave me her cell number. I called, but she was busy unpacking. She promised to call later.

True to her word, the next day Daystar phoned. She asked me to email the narrative I'd kept in my journal to her. She said she'd look it over and get back to me with a recommendation.

By then, it was the last week of October. We had returned to the every other week schedule with Britt rotating between Sheila and me. So for the first time in three and a half months, Britt returned to my house. It was the week before Halloween.

The events of the previous nine months had had a profound effect on all of us and caused us all to do a great deal of soul searching. Sheila took refuge in an evangelical approach to Christianity, while I delved more deeply into things I was reading and learning about metaphysics. I was desperate for some divine power source that could protect Brittany from the demonic entities that were trying to repossess her body, claiming they wanted to steal her soul.

I don't believe the method used to reach out to and contact Divinity is as important as the actual link or hook-up to Divinity, the Universe, or God. I am firmly convinced that whatever works well for you in your spiritual quest is what is best.

My study of Wicca and Paganism in general focused very much on their important holidays, the most important of which is Halloween—the Celtic New Year. According to Druidry (a religion or spirituality based on the priests of the Celts, called Druids), Samhain (Halloween) is the time of year when the veil between this world and the otherworld is the thinnest.

Now Brittany had always celebrated Halloween in a big way, just like all kids. It was always a huge holiday for her mother, too. Back when we were married, Sheila always made a really big deal of decorating the house for Halloween and preparing for the big Halloween parties we'd have. And that was back before I cared very much about it one way or the other.

But Halloween was upon us, and Britt was extremely excited. She decorated the house and prepared her costume. (She and Dave were going trick or treating in the neighborhood.) Things actually did seem to be getting back to normal, despite Brittany's claims of demonic entities trying to return.

Then she started channeling again for the first time in months (with the exception of a couple of visits from Spence). The night before Halloween, we were preparing to go to a sort of staged haunted house at a theatre. Billed as a "séance to summon the Bell Witch," it was actually a play *about* a séance to summon Tennessee's most famous spirit. Anyway, we sat in the kitchen eating dinner before the show, and that old, familiar, spacey look came across Britt's face. Her eyes rolled back into her head, and she sort of zoned out for a couple of seconds. When she came back, she looked at me like she didn't recognize me, turning her head from side to side as if trying to figure out who or what I might be. Then she made the gurgling, giggling sounds a baby makes and began playing in her food instead of eating it.

If I'd never seen her channel before, I probably would have totally freaked out. However, from my experiences with Britt channeling months earlier, I knew to remain calm, be friendly and loving to this new entity, and perhaps try to communicate with it.

Apparently this was the spirit of a very young baby, so I got up and hugged it and told them that I loved them. After a few moments of attempted conversation, I realized the entity didn't really understand me—although the hugs seemed to comfort it. But it was unable to communicate verbally. Still playing in the food, Brittany attempted to throw a few green peas; however, I gently demonstrated that this was not acceptable and would not be allowed.

After a bit more clowning with the food, the baby stood up in her chair. Afraid she might hurt herself, I gently coaxed Britt down. Then she giggled and ran into the living room, stopping at the foot of the stairs. She eyed the top step as if to toddle up, so rather than let her dash up the stairs in a wobble, I stood between Britt and the stairway. Then she did a perfectly natural thing for a baby to do, but it was an action that took me totally by surprise—and totally embarrassed Brittany when she came to.

Our infant guest stood there in front of the living room door and urinated. With urine streaming down her leg, Britt/Baby laughed and giggled—even sloshing her feet in the liquid. Luckily, she stood on a 4' x 4' entrance area between the front door and the stairway that was covered in tile rather than carpet.

By now my mother heard the commotion, came into the living room, and held Brittany still while I ran upstairs for some towels. After cleaning Britt and the floor, I asked the entity in my most pleasant voice (although, I admit, I was a bit shaken) if Brittany couldn't come back—always being careful to assure the entity we loved it and enjoyed meeting it. Britt/Baby nodded in the affirmative (was a part of our communication telepathic?), and my daughter slumped to the ground.

When she came to, I told Britt what had happened: food slinging, urine and all.

"Oh, gross!" she exclaimed and was totally mortified by the incident.

After she'd had a bath, we proceeded on to the Bell Witch séance play.

It occurred to me that with the veil between dimensions being so thin at that time of year, Brittany was going to be very vulnerable to entities wanting to pop in and have their say. I had figured Britt would feel much safer if I could get a shaman like Daystar to cast a protective spell to keep wandering beasties from jumping onboard during Samhain, much as the baby entity had. But it was already Halloween eve, and there was no time to find anyone to do this. So with very little practical experience or knowledge in witchcraft, I decided to cast the spell myself. I had had the beginner's course in Wicca, had read books, and had started my own Book of Shadows (a sort of personal manual, including historical facts about Paganism, definitions, and spells). I did not truly feel qualified to do this, but it seemed to me at the time I had no other alternatives.

I took a deep breath, composed a spell, cast a magic circle, and cast the spell before we left the house. The spell I designed follows:

"Mighty Goddess, protect thy servant Brittany this night from any who'd try to enter her Light."

Britt seemed a bit surprised at her old dad casting spells, but it definitely pleased her that I'd go to this extreme to help. She was noticeably relieved. After the incident with the intruding baby entity, she had been anxious and apprehensive—dreading, no doubt, a recurrence of the events of the preceding January. However, the spell seemed to give her confidence, and a peace and calm came over her that I hadn't seen lately. I sincerely believe that in this case, the intent is what really mattered and not the act itself. So if all the spell actually did was to encourage her to keep her guard up, then it was worth it.

On Halloween day itself, there were no further incidents of channeling. Britt and Dave prepared their costumes for their evening of trick or treating.

Before they left with Dave's friend Anthony and his girlfriend in Anthony's car, I took their photos. Then off they went, with Britt seeming to be in a very good and relaxed mood.

The next day Britt confided in me that several times during the evening's merriment, she had strongly felt the tug of the demonic forces that had so tightly gripped her months earlier. But she resisted and said she felt the protective spell had really worked.

That Sunday, Britt returned to her mother's to spend her week. Meanwhile, I had been contacted by a local theatre group about taking a part in a holiday play, *An O. Henry Christmas*. Rehearsals were to begin that week, Monday through Thursday, 7:00 to 9:30 p.m. I hesitated about taking the role, because I was worried about leaving Britt alone if the channeling and/or possessions resumed. But when I learned this was going to be a short rehearsal schedule, I decided to give it a shot—after I asked Brittany and Mima both if they thought they could manage. Britt loves theatre, and she was eager for me to take the role. And she would only be at my house two of the weeks I'd be rehearsing.

Daystar did call me back after she'd read the narrative. She was very supportive and wanted to help in any way she could. And she was particularly put out with me for not telling her about the possession back in January, insisting she would have been happy to conduct the exorcism. I should have contacted her, and I wish that I had. But I tried to explain to Daystar about the importance of including Sheila's belief system into the exorcism and my apprehension about her disapproval of Daystar's avowed Paganism. I was certain that Britt's mother wouldn't have condoned an exorcism performed by a non-Christian. Laurel had been a compromise candidate in many respects, but now it seemed that what she had done hadn't been entirely effective.

Chapter 12

The Voodoo Exorcism

Daystar told me about a friend of hers named Hans who was a psychic and had been trained to be a Zulu *sangoma*—what laymen might refer to as a "witch doctor." Hans was an Afrikaner from South Africa, where he had been trained as a sangoma since the age of four when his mother died and his father had placed him into the hands of a trusted black employee who just happened to be a sangoma himself. The Zulu immediately recognized an incredible amount of psychic ability in this young white child, so he inducted the boy into the Zulu Pagan religion and taught him everything he knew.

Daystar felt certain that Hans could rid Brittany of any demons that might still be there and prevent any more from entering, but probably more importantly, he could teach her to use her own psychic abilities.

"A child like Brittany only comes along once or twice in a lifetime," said Daystar, "and I think Hans will be anxious to work with her." She gave me his phone number and told me she'd call him and let him know I'd be contacting him.

That evening I called Hans. Daystar had indeed already talked with him, so he said he'd be happy to work with Brittany. But first he wanted to talk to me. So we made an appointment to get together that Saturday afternoon.

I took a hard copy of the original narrative of the "holy water incident" with me, but basically relayed the whole story once again, verbally. He seemed confident he could help. I expressed my gratitude but told him I wouldn't be able to pay him much, since I was far from well-off. Hans said that money would not be an issue, because mainly he just wanted the opportunity to work with Brittany. He felt like it was a chance for him to "give back to the universe." Someone had once helped him develop his abilities, and now he would have the chance to help someone else. I liked this young man immediately. He was only twenty-six years old but appeared extremely knowledgeable about metaphysics and occult phenomena.

We made an appointment for him to meet her the following week after I picked Britt up from school.

That next week, Britt came back to my house. As I drove her to school Monday morning, I told her about Hans. I didn't know how she'd react. I half expected her to just tell me she didn't want anything to do with this new weird scheme of mine. However, she was extremely interested and very much wanted to meet him. She seemed very excited about the possibility of him helping her develop her own psychic abilities. I told her that we had an appointment with Hans for Wednesday afternoon.

"Can't we go see him sooner than that?" she asked. I was delighted to see her so enthusiastic but assured her that Wednesday would be soon enough.

"Call him and see if we can't go today."

I asked her what was so urgent, and she just replied that "weird things had been happening at school" and she was scared. She said she had begun seeing spirits at school. I reiterated that Hans was pretty busy, and I doubted he could see us any sooner than Wednesday anyway.

As I was preparing to go to rehearsals on that Monday evening, I noticed a couple of times that Britt had a vacant look on her face. When asked if she was alright, she'd seem not to hear for a few seconds, then shake her head and snap back to reality. After Dave came over, she seemed a bit more alert but I still wasn't certain whether I should go to rehearsals or not.

Then, as all four of us were standing in the kitchen, Brittany collapsed on the floor. I rushed to her side just as she came to. She looked at me like she didn't know who I was, so I called her name, hoping to retrieve her from wherever she'd psychically gone. The entity just stared back at me with a rather malicious grin on its face.

"Brittany, Brittany," I called. "Come back, now."

"Fuck you" was its only reply. Then it started growling and hissing.

I took her by the wrists and told Dave to hold her legs as we pinned her to the ground. I developed a new and unexpected respect for Brittany's boyfriend at that moment. A lot of kids would have gone screaming out into the street, but he kept a level head and seemed eager to help. Mima was standing over us shouting at the demon to "leave this child's body in the name of Jesus Christ." At the time, invoking the name of Jesus wasn't the route I would have taken—but I was glad to see Mima participate and eager for any divine intervention we could get.

I was starting to realize that the important thing in exorcising any entity wasn't in engaging *it* in any way. What was more important was to recall Britt from wherever she'd gone and get her to reclaim what was rightfully hers. So I started singing "Dixie"—that song from her childhood that had brought her back from the abyss back in January.

And it worked. After only a few verses, the light came back into her eyes and I heard the magic words, "Daddy? Daddy?"

Mima and Dave stayed with her while I went to rehearsals, and everything returned to normal.

Although I had kept a pretty detailed journal of the events of Brittany's actual possession, subsequent exorcism, and the ten months or so afterward—I did not make an entry describing the second exorcism conducted by the sangoma, Hans. I always assumed I'd go back and put this very important episode into my journal, but that never happened. So here I am over a decade and a half later trying to remember exactly what happened. The minute details you've found in the rest of the story, I'm afraid, just can't be replicated to describe this particular episode. Summarizing the events is simply the best I can do. As subsequent events over the years have proven, Hans's exorcism was far more significant than I realized at the time.

I picked Brittany up after school that Wednesday and we drove to Hans's apartment. Hans lived on the other side of town with his wife and her son from a previous marriage. When we got there, his wife answered the door and led us to the living room. Hans had gone to the school to pick her son up. She brought us soft drinks and we chatted about the various Pagan artifacts that decorated their home. There were a couple of cats wandering around and Brittany and I are always happy to get a chance to play with cats.

After a few more minutes, Hans and his stepson arrived talking about the rugby match they were preparing for. Hans coached a rugby team for the kids after school, so I learned more about this very non-American sport that day than I'd ever known before. Being an Afrikaner from Johannesburg, Hans has a thick accent that takes a bit of getting used to—so the Rugby discussion gave us a chance to get to know each other and also for Britt and me to adjust to his accent.

Michelle's son went to his room to do his homework, and she took the car to run errands. Hans led us into the kitchen where Britt and I sat at the table as he gathered together the voodoo paraphernalia he'd be using. There was a little leather bag of small bones that he would cast out on the table, some kind of incense, and feathers, which he'd use to direct the billows of sage.

There was nothing really spooky or otherworldly about anything Hans did. But then I'd never witnessed anything remotely like a voodoo ceremony before. He moved a chair away from the table into the center of the room and had Brittany sit there. He told her just to relax and not try to block anything. Then he took sea salt and encircled her chair with it. I'd filled Hans in on all the channeling Britt had been doing the last few months, so he'd be ready if that happened. He chanted something in a language I did not recognize, but I assume because of where he'd gotten his training that it was Zulu. He told us he was calling on his ancestors to protect us. He lit the sage and directed it toward Brittany, cast the bones out on the table, and said something else in Zulu.

By now, Brittany's head had tipped to the side and her eyes had closed. Hans demanded to speak with whatever spirits were in her at the time. His demeanor was considerably more confrontational than Laurel's. But then I figured different psychics or shamans have different styles.

I hadn't expected this to be so much another exorcism as a minor cleansing—kind of a tune-up maybe. Laurel had gotten the big bads out, so this would be like a booster shot.

However, he had told us earlier that he wasn't certain all the demonic spirits had left that night of the exorcism. He demanded that the entity speak to him. Brittany's eyes reopened and she straightened her neck. She looked at me and smiled.

"Well hello there, Bill," she said in that Irish brogue we had come to recognize as Spence. "And who would this be?" she asked pointing to Hans.

"That's Hans," I replied. "He's a shaman, and he's trying to make sure no more unwanted spirits or demons get into Brittany."

"Well now, lad, that'd be my job, don't you know? Don't you worry, I'll be takin' good care of her," said Spence in his usual chipper voice.

"I'll be the judge of that," replied Hans.

It soon became clear than Hans did not regard Spence as the friendly Irish guardian angel that he'd been claiming to be. Laurel had totally agreed that Spence was basically who he said he was (a fallen angel who had returned to the light), and that he was a protecting force in Brittany's life—even if he might not exactly be a guardian angel. She felt that he was, at the very least, one of her guides.

But it seemed that Hans wasn't buying into it. He challenged Spence to offer up some kind of proof that he was indeed a positive entity. Spence seemed quite offended by this and stubbornly refused to answer most of Hans's questions.

Not having written this incident down in the journal, the details of the conversation between Hans and Spence are floating around out there somewhere in the ether. I can remember that the discourse was quite contentious. Hans kept demanding evidence from Spence to prove his guardian angel status, and Spence resolutely stood by his guns proclaiming that he had no need to prove anything to Hans or anyone else. The atmosphere was more than a little heated. All the while, Hans circled Brittany as she sat in her chair in the middle of the room. She spoke with Spence's voice in weaker and weaker tones as he wore her down with his accusations intermingled with chants in Zulu, waving his bag of bones in her face and directing burning sage and incense around her head with that feather.

Hans continually kept asking Spence to state his "true name"—not Spence and not the angel name of Kalikalik he had given Laurel. At first Spence, just as adamantly, refused to even qualify this with an answer. At one point, they were practically shouting at each other—with Hans accusing Spence of being a lying demonic entity, and Spence proclaiming his innocence and purporting to be Britt's guardian angel. But after nearly an hour of this back-and-forth match of wills, Spence started to weaken.

As Hans drove his accusations home, his voice became louder and louder—and Spence's voice became weaker and weaker. He seemed to have lost his will to fight. Over the preceding ten months or so, the Spence entity had almost become a member of our family—more of a friend than just some personality that Brittany channeled. As Hans continued to badger his witness like a prosecuting attorney, I felt more and more sympathy for my new Irish friend. I asked Hans if he really felt this was necessary, but by then he was so wrapped up in the righteousness of his mission that he barely paid any attention to me. I felt very sorry for Spence, but my main objective was to help my daughter—so if Hans believed this was the way to relieve her distress, then I was just going to have to trust his judgment.

Hans continued to ask Spence for his true name, and Spence kept asserting that his name was either Spence or Kalikalik, the name he'd given Laurel. This seemed odd to me. I mean, why would this be so important even *if* Spence were a demonic entity as Hans suspected? I learned later that most exorcists and demonologists believe that if you can get a demon to state their true name given them by God, then you have power over them. Once you've successfully identified a demon, supposedly they *must* leave the body of the person they're possessing if they are commanded in the name of the deity you believe in. At least, that's the theory.

So Hans continued to hound the Spence entity for his true name. Spence's resolve not to give out any more information than he already had was becoming decidedly weaker. Hans loomed over Brittany-as-Spence. He never touched Spence/Brittany, but his presence was overwhelming.

"Again, give me your real name," said Hans forcefully. The entity Spence looked at me as if pleading for help, then looked away from both of us.

"I am 'nothing,'" it said.

"What?" asked Hans. "Say it again!"

"I am 'nothing,'" replied Spence, now in total defeat.

Hans seemed victorious, as if he had solved a Rubik's cube he'd been working on for hours. "Leave this child now!" he thundered. Britt's eyes closed, and her head tilted over to the side as if she'd suddenly fallen asleep.

Hans then gently touched Brittany's face. "Brittany, come back," he said softly.

Brittany came out of the trance and looked at us with bewilderment. "Is it over?" she asked. "What happened?"

Without going into much detail, Hans told her he had gotten the entity out—and that Spence was actually a demon pretending to be her guardian angel.

Hans then asked us if we would care for anything to drink, but as I recall it, his wife came into the kitchen about the time he was pouring Brittany a soft drink with some domestic emergency demanding Hans's immediate attention. So the session came to a rather abrupt end when Hans had to leave. He told us to call him if we had any more questions or if anything else happened.

Britt finished her drink, and we were soon back in the car headed home. Since Brittany didn't remember 95 percent of what had happened, I tried to fill her in on the way.

As we drove along in my black '89 Sterling, I tried to explain to her what Hans had done and said and why he seemed to think Spence was the actual demon. I mentioned that with all the pleasant and often comic interactions the entire family had had with the affable Irish-sounding spirit, I was highly skeptical about Hans's conclusions about Spence—especially since Laurel had also been convinced that Spence was basically who he said he was. The family had come to enjoy having Spence around during his impromptu visits. He was funny, gracious, and seemingly Brittany's staunchest ally during her times of need.

Brittany agreed, and was actually quite appalled that Hans thought Spence was a (or *the*) demon. He seemed to have been such an enormous help in a time when we all felt so alone, seeing Spence as the actual cause of the problem was just too much to accept. We frankly felt the trip to see Hans had been a waste of time, and Brittany was afraid that her friend, Spence, might never come back.

But Spence did come back. Just a couple of days later, Brittany came down the stairs with a huge grin on her face, speaking in the Irish brogue with which we had all become familiar. When asked how he felt about Hans's voodoo exorcism, Spence just laughed it off, saying he thought at the time it would be best to simply "play along" with Hans.

"Sure and it didn't seem he was going to give up," Spence said with a laugh, "so I humored him. He was determined to chalk it up as a win for the voodoo team, so I just gave him the game, faked a whimper and went on me way."

Spence would continue to make sporadic appearances in our lives during the next four years—usually only showing up at times when Brittany would be particularly stressed out about something. Essentially, he did seem to be playing the part of something of a guardian, so we basically just accepted him in that or some beneficial role. But he didn't seem to be omniscient, so I eventually decided he wasn't cut from angel material—when asked questions of world import, he never gave an answer approaching

Edgar Casey's sleeping prophet. Spence always seemed to be more interested in what was in the refrigerator.

He was funny, and he was immensely entertaining, but he just wasn't interested in sharing the secrets of the universe—if he even knew any of them. I finally assumed Spence was really just a disembodied human spirit because he frequently mentioned his wife from a life he'd lived in Ireland as a shoemaker. According to Spence, angels sometimes lived in human form just to "get the feel of what bein' human is like." I was pretty sure that was just a bit of blarney coming from an Irish spirit who missed his wife.

Spence played a relatively important role in our lives for that first year after the possession, but by the time Brittany was eighteen or so, we rarely heard from him.

Psychic Training Maybe Not So Free

Hans had initially promised to work with Brittany for free just to have the chance to help her develop her psychic abilities. However when I asked him later about tutoring her, he indicated there would be a fee. He made his living from his skills in voodoo, so I totally understand why he needed to charge. We simply weren't in a position to pay, so that tutelage never happened. But since Brittany nor I believed that Hans's conclusions about Spence had been correct anyway, it seemed best to disregard that option.

Airborne China and Unsettled Cabinets

A few weeks after the cleansing with Hans, Britt and I had just returned from visiting my mother at her apartment for Grandparent's Day. After we arrived at home, I worked a couple of hours on my weekly theatre review, while Britt watched TV. I finished up and went upstairs to get ready for bed. Britt went into the kitchen to take the nightly regimen of pills the doctors had put her on during her stay in the hospital.

I heard a piercing scream from the kitchen and rushed downstairs. Brittany was standing at the far end of the room by the kitchen table, shaking like a leaf and still screaming and crying.

"The cabinet doors started flying open by themselves. Dishes and bowls were flying out!" she screamed.

She went on to describe how the apparition of an old woman (whom she said vaguely resembled her grandmother) had appeared in the kitchen. The apparition was laughing, as she opened and slammed the doors to the cabinets. Then dishes and bowls started flying of their own accord out into thin air, dancing about at six or seven feet above the floor. She said most of them flew back into the cabinet, but one bowl hurled itself down onto the floor.

Indeed, there was a shattered bowl on the floor in front of the cabinet doors. Brittany was completely on the other side of the room fifteen feet away.

This particular set of dishes is extremely durable, made by a French company of virtually indestructible colored glass rather than china. I'm terribly clumsy and have dropped various pieces onto the linoleum in the kitchen—and the dishes are nearly impossible to break. The bowl on the floor at my feet must have hit the linoleum with incredible force, or it simply would not have broken into tiny pieces like that.

My first objective was to try and calm Brittany down. I hugged her and relayed some information I'd just read the previous week about telekinetic energy in a book entitled *Psychic Connections: A*

Journey into the Mysterious World of PSI by Lois Duncan and Dr. William Roll.

The book concerns the study of logical parapsychology as opposed to things mystic and supernatural. The concept of there being scientific, physical laws that could be applied to events that psychics and mystics of various religions have claimed for centuries to be supernatural appealed to me. This particular book was a real revelation to me, and it seemed to explain many of the bizarre things that had been happening in my household and specifically to my daughter.

There's a detailed account of an investigation by Dr. Roll of supposed poltergeist activity in the home of teenager Tina Resch. Physical objects were observed by family members and friends (and later scientists under laboratory conditions) to rise up of their own accord and fly across the room. Dr. Roll even has a photograph of a hand-held telephone sailing through the air in front of Tina who is seated in a chair. What was first thought to be ghostly activity was eventually diagnosed as intense telekinetic ability on the part of Tina. The fourteen-year-old proved quite adept under laboratory conditions at moving forks, spoons, hair brushes, and other small objects up to fifteen feet through the air as scientists observed and took notes.

Tina fit the typical profile of a telekinetic young girl. Those most often observed to have telekinetic ability appear to be teenaged girls who have an unusual amount of real or perceived stress in their lives. She was an adopted child who lived in a household in which a number of foster children were always present. They were usually much younger than her, and she felt slighted and neglected by her parents who seemed to require her to follow the same rules as the younger children. She was also having difficulties with her boyfriend at the time. Often the telekinetic activity was directed at the foster children, e.g., their toys would break or the TV show they were watching would turn itself off. Once the TV even came on while it was unplugged. At the dinner table, the chairs of the foster children would often slip backward, leaving the children sitting on the floor. The lights would also come on and off, with observers even seeing the switches flip up and down and no one causing the activity.

Anyway, I tried to explain a little about telekinetic activity and some of the things I had read in the book to Brittany. I tried to make her see that we may have been wrong all along about there being malevolent spirits lurking out there. I said that what she saw might just be concentrated energy—sometimes lingering from the past after traumatic events, or sometimes even projected by our own minds. Dr. Roll explained that there are cases in which persons with psychic ability have projected ghost-like figures, which other people have actually seen.

I tried to explain that this didn't make what had been happening to her any less real. According to the things I was reading about parapsychology, these things actually happened—at least on some level. Viewing the events as parapsychological activity could explain strange and frightening things in rational, scientific terms.

I came to believe that the things happening to us might someday have logical, scientific explanations. But while viewing the incidents plaguing our family under a more scientific microscope helped me understand and cope with them, I'm not so sure that Brittany was much convinced. She showed interest and politely listened to my revelations, but I really can't say how thoroughly she bought into the whole parapsychological explanation at the time.

Chapter 13
Paranormal Incidents Through the Years

After about ten months, most of the paranormal incidents ceased—at least on a daily basis. Brittany returned to school, albeit a different one (she didn't want to go back to the same school where she would be around the aforementioned ex-boyfriend). I continued writing for the newspaper and directing and acting in plays in the Nashville area. My mother continued to stay with us during the weeks Brittany was at my house, commuting back and forth to her apartment downtown on the weeks Britt stayed with her mother.

Paranormally, things were much more peaceful. I believe that her experience with the other side had been so traumatic that Brittany consciously put up a mental barrier to block all things paranormal. For a few years, life was relatively ordinary. She graduated from high school and then enrolled at Tennessee Technological College in Nashville to study to be an aesthetician. She actually wanted to become a makeup artist, but aesthetician was about as close a match as she could find and not have to travel to New York or L.A. It was a two-year course, and she was in her final quarter when she started dating a young man named Kevin who worked for the U.S. Post Office. They fell in love and decided to get married, then Britt quit school before graduation. Britt and Kevin bought a house near her mother, and life went on. Sometimes she worked, and sometimes she didn't. Luckily, Kevin made enough money that it wasn't absolutely essential for Brittany to work.

Once they were married, I didn't see nearly as much of Brittany. Paranormal occurrences continued during the next five years for her and separately for me at my house. But they were sporadic and for the most part harmless. A few events seemed noteworthy enough to write down at the time, so I'll try to summarize a few of the incidents I did jot down in a separate file on my computer.

Getting Reception Without a Paranormal "Antenna"

Laurel had said that Brittany was the psychic magnet making paranormal things happen at my house. The first time Laurel went through my condo, she said, "The house is not haunted. Brittany is pulling these entities in." So I took that ball and ran with it for many years. I just assumed Britt was the antenna that was attracting paranormal events, which had proved oh so less than entertaining.

However, that didn't explain the sporadic paranormal events that occurred here after Britt married and left home. Granted, the magnitude and intensity of the events were infinitely greater when she was here—but sometimes, inexplicable things happened anyway. I couldn't help but wonder why, so I did a little research. I knew that the condos were built in 1985, but I wondered if maybe there had been some creepy old Victorian house full of spirits here before. But it turned out the condos were built on land that had been a horse farm—another dead-end street.

But since my paranormal events were usually not bothersome (and often just interesting or even mildly funny), I didn't give them too much thought.

Electronic Voice Phenomena on My Eighties Answering Machine

One Sunday afternoon a couple of years after Brittany left home, I was sitting at my computer writing my weekly theatre review. There was no one in the condo but me. (After Brittany got married, my mom moved back to her apartment full time, only dropping by for the occasional visit.)

The phone rang, and my old eighties answering machine picked up the call. The messages usually sound crystal clear, but this one was almost overpowered by background static. Just above the static I could hear a tiny voice say, "Hello, hello? Why can't anyone hear me? I'm talking and I'm talking, so why doesn't anyone hear me?" The voice actually sounded a bit like Brittany, so I leaned over and picked up the receiver.

"Brittany, is that you?" I responded. "Is something wrong?"

The voice that answered me sounded far away, lost and desperate. I could tell now that it definitely wasn't Brittany.

"Where are you?" it asked. "Where did you go? Why can't anyone hear me? I don't know where I am."

"Who is this? Hello? Are you sure you have the right number?" I asked.

"Hello, hello, please answer me," it pleaded. "Someone, anyone … are you there?"

"Brittany, is that you? What's wrong?" Then the line just went dead. Not like the person on the other side had hung up, but just suddenly *not there.*

I was more than a little rattled by this odd call from someone with a voice so similar to Britt's—someone who was obviously lost and in a great deal of distress. I dialed Brittany's home number. It rang quite a long time, but she eventually picked up and answered with a deeply sleepy voice. She said she and Kevin were taking a nap. They'd been up very late the night before and had been asleep when I called. I told her about the call I'd just gotten, but she didn't know anything about it. It obviously hadn't been her.

Was this an example of an EVP (electronic voice phenomena) coming through my phone and answering machine? Of course, I have no evidence whatsoever to back that up—but that was frankly the impression I got. I've heard of EVPs coming through over shortwave radios and even just regular radios. But I never hear of anyone picking up an EVP over an old phone's answering machine. I kept the message on my machine for months, playing it for Brittany and a few others. But the power went out one night in a storm and it (along with all my other messages) was lost. My fault. I knew that the first time we had a power failure, it would be lost. I kept meaning to record it onto a tape player, so I'd have a backup—but of course I didn't. But if I had to bet on what I thought that tiny voice was, so lost and so alone, I'd put my money on an EVP from the other side.

Gee, If They Could Just Be Taught to Clean House

During the five years Brittany was married to Kevin, she had numerous jobs, including being a caregiver for the elderly, working as a clerk in several retail stores, and working as a housekeeper for several maid services.

After Britt got married and my mom moved out, I'd hire one of those maid services to come in and get the house more or less presentable. Since Britt had been working for a maid service, it seemed like a good idea to pay her to clean my place up. I get a clean house, and she earns a few bucks. Win-win.

At the time, I was directing a play I had written called *Otto* about a real-life Holocaust survivor and spent most of my nights in rehearsal. In the midst of rehearsing a scene, I got a frantic call from her on my cell phone.

"I was at your place cleaning up, but weird things started happening," she said. "I had to get out of there. I'm sorry. I got part of the house cleaned up, but I just can't go back with nobody there."

She said that after she had cleaned the upstairs, she went down to the kitchen to evaluate what needed to be done there. The cleaning supplies she needed for this were out in her car, so she went out to get them. When she came back, all the kitchen cabinet doors had been flung wide open, and the six kitchen chairs were stacked at several odd angles atop the table. Not having to be told twice that someone or something didn't want her to upset the sanctity of my home by cleaning it, Brittany grabbed her cleaning supplies and made a quick retreat back to her car. She didn't pull over to call me until she was several blocks away.

"I didn't even want to be sitting in the parking lot," she said. "Something was in there, and I didn't know whether it could come out and get me."

Brittany needed the money, so even a skeptic would have to admit that she wouldn't leave before the job was done.

Since holding rehearsals was my responsibility, I couldn't leave twenty-five actors standing around scratching their heads while I rushed off to play ghostbusters. So I went back to work and resumed rehearsing. I told my co-director and good friend, Rodney Pickle, what had happened. He's a very religious/spiritual man and didn't doubt me for a second. He had known Brittany for several years and had even acted with her in a play I wrote. He knew she was credible and not crazy. He listened attentively when I told him what she'd just relayed to me, and then told me a couple of ghost stories that had happened to him over the years.

After we finished rehearsals that evening, I drove home. If this had happened eight or ten years earlier, I would have had to deal with the fear factor as I unlocked the door and went into a dark house that I knew had been the sight of paranormal activity just a few hours before. However, I was just mad. Some interdimensional beastie had once again disrupted my life, scared the wits out of my daughter, prevented her from making some extra money, and even had the audacity to touch my things.

But as I turned the doorknob and stepped in, I remembered something Laurel had told me years earlier. Exhibiting anger is not the most effective reaction when dealing with the beasties. These beings feed on anger the same way they do fear. Anger and fear just make them stronger. Laurel also used to say that they hate being laughed at—just as most bullies do.

But once in the kitchen, I could see what had spooked Brittany. Sure enough, the chairs were all stacked on the kitchen table, with some upside down, some right side up, some at odd angles. Chair legs were resting on the seats of other chairs (often in precarious positions)—and the doors and drawers to all the kitchen cabinets were wide open.

Remembering what Laurel had said, I decided to make a joke out of the whole thing. "Very clever! Great job of redecorating the kitchen," I mocked. "But why can't you learn how to do something useful like wash the dishes or do housework? Don't you think it's about time you earned your keep around here?"

I was genuinely more angry than scared. I had missed the chance to have my house cleaned, and Brittany had missed out on earning a little extra money merely because some screwball spirit had decided to play a prank. After years of being hassled by formless entities, I had about reached the end of my patience. That night I went to bed the same as usual, as if nothing had happened. But sometime during the night, the TV in my bedroom came on by itself. I woke up and said:

"Will you just stop it? I have things to do tomorrow, even if you don't! I'd like to get a little sleep!" I've had insomnia since I was a teenager, so sleep is precious to me. I am never amused at anything, even a wacky spirit, that causes me to lose sleep more than I do all on my own. Luckily, I was somehow actually able to go back to sleep that night.

Rodney asked me the next night at rehearsal what I had found at home. When I told him about the devastation in the kitchen and the TV turning itself on, he said if it were him he'd just move. But by then, I'd become used to things bumping and thumping in the night.

Traveling Teddy

Then there was the case of the nomadic teddy bear. Somewhere along the way, I had given Brittany a very small (eight inches), white teddy bear with a red ribbon around its neck for Valentine's

Day. After she got married and left home, I kept finding Brittany's little white teddy at various locations throughout the house. I was living there alone, so I knew I hadn't moved it—and if the cats had moved it in a game of "swat the fluffy," it would have shown up on the floor flopped over on its side (or worse). But I would find the little bear neatly placed first on one bookshelf and then another. Sometimes it would make a guest appearance on my desk. Occasionally, it would materialize on the kitchen table. But it was always sitting straight up, as if it had been put on display. That went on, sporadically, for about a year. I wondered if it might be the spirit of a child who just liked playing with the teddy bear. After a year of finding the stuffed toy on first one shelf, bookcase, table, or counter and then the other, I got a bit tired of the game and put the teddy bear in a drawer. Frankly, things were starting to get a little creepy. I felt like I was playing with a child I couldn't see. Apparently, this spirit didn't have the ability to get it out of a drawer, so this particular phenomenon never happened again. I never did really figure out the rhyme or reason to it.

Adventures in Electricity

My little invisible friends also seemed to like to manipulate electrical gizmos, e.g., radios, TVs, and occasionally the can opener. Hearing the can opener open an invisible can while you're trying to eat dinner can be more than a bit unsettling. But after everything we'd been through, I took these minor irritations with a grain of salt—and usually just fashioned some kind of wisecrack about it.

The TV turning itself on in the middle of the night got to be a fairly common occurrence after Brittany got married. Not really scary, but extremely irritating.

I often wondered if the spirit found my lack of any frantic reaction to its pranks a bit frustrating. It had gotten used to scaring Brittany with these parlor tricks, and I'm sure it took some kind of perverse pleasure in that. But with me making jokes about its paranormal antics, I probably had a very unfulfilled spirit lurking about.

Showering with Casper

I always listen to the radio when I'm in the shower and getting ready for the day. One morning, I cranked up the radio, selected a political talk show on the Public Broadcasting Service network, climbed into the tub and pulled the curtain. The water was soothing, and the reception on the radio was crystal clear. The announcer was discussing the president's recent State of the Union address with commentary by some local political science college professor.

Then the perfectly clear radio reception turned to static. This, in and of itself, is not that unusual. Irritating, but not the end of the world. I listened to the static for a few seconds, debating whether I should get out of the tub and adjust the selector knob (not a pleasant alternative considering the January cold), or just finish my shower and endure the static. Still had to wash my hair, so maybe more static than I could stand—especially considering how loud the radio was. Decisions, decisions.

But then the lights went out. With the static still grinding on my every nerve, I couldn't very well blame my light deficiency on a power outage. Static takes juice, too.

Then it occurred to me that my resident spirit might have caused this. Assuming my electrical spirit was manipulating the current, I said out loud:

"Very funny. Static, that's great. Alright. But you have to listen to it too. Dumbass!"

I figured all the reverberations and shrill audio frequencies had to be as unpleasant for Casper as they were for me. Fine, but also—I couldn't see to finish the shower.

"Alright, Casper, you may like the darkness, but I like to be able to see the soap!"

Then things got even more interesting. The lights suddenly came back on and a new listening alternative presented itself when the radio switched stations all by itself. The station had gone from the world of PBS talk to the above-described static. Now it re-tuned itself to the local jazz station—from 90.3 to 88. Instead of wisecracking political remarks, the broadcast pendulum had swung to total audio-fuzz, and then to Billie Holiday singing "God Bless the Child." I have a pretty old-fashioned stereo/radio: AM/FM, DVD, two separate speakers. Nothing fancy. No remote anything—nothing I could have accomplished from inside the shower.

There was no one else in the condo. Just me. The radio is jumping stations like crazy; the lights go out; the radio is still crazy; and then the lights come back on. This particular combination of audio fits-and-starts, complete with a light show, had never happened before in the fourteen years I'd lived here. It seemed something more was going on here than personal hygiene. Static was one thing, because the station might have slipped by itself (I suppose—I really don't know anything about how radio works). But there I stood, listening to Billie Holiday and belting out her song, clear as a bell. I briefly considered running out into the parking lot dripping wet. But instead, I decided to sing along with her—washing my hair, singing "God Bless the Child" and wondering what the hell was coming next.

Billie finished her song, and then the jazz station started playing a modern jazz number I'd never heard before. Apparently Casper wasn't too fond of this little ditty. Then the station switched back to my original selection, the political talk show. The political pundits were back, my hair was washed, I was squeaky clean, and Casper had once again had a chance to stretch his/her static electrical muscles.

Not a bad shower, all things considered. But I much prefer showering alone.

Waya

Early one morning around two a.m., I was awakened by a clattering noise downstairs that sounded kind of like pans banging together. I heard it with my ears, but it also seemed to be inside my head. But whatever it was, I knew it wasn't a normal sound that should be coming from my kitchen at two a.m.

I jumped up and went downstairs. Looking back, I realize I should have been more cautious. What if it had been a burglar? But my mind doesn't think like that. I'm the least paranoid person you'll ever meet.

When I got to the kitchen, I did not see a pile of pans the cats had knocked out of the cabinets. There were no pans or dishes or anything else that was out of place.

What I did see, though, was more than a bit unnerving. The image only lasted for maybe ten or fifteen seconds, but standing in front of the sink looking back at me was what appeared to be a bare-chested, extremely tall, Native American man with long hair and some kind of colorful headdress. He was holding something that looked like a thick wooden drumstick. I was not scared. My reaction was reminiscent of the time I had seen the spirit of a woman in forties' clothing at the foot of my bed, or when I had seen the spirit of the old lady in a pillbox hat in the cemetery. Like them, this one appeared transparent—totally fleshed out in three-dimensional detail, but you could see right through him. He had black hair, brown eyes, and some kind of colorful design painted on his chest. Something about the look in his eyes reminded me of a wolf—calculating yet wary, as if planning its next three moves in advance. He looked back at me and nodded slowly, as if to say, "Ah, so you see me. Good then."

And then he was gone. Was that him beating the stainless steel metal sink with that drumstick creating a sound like pans clanking together? Maybe. But regardless of his purpose, he sure got my attention. And I had the feeling that just letting me know he was around was the gist of his visit.

He did not, in any way, look like he meant me harm—nor did I feel threatened. But I couldn't help but shake my head when he disappeared. It was, I think, some kind of primal reaction—maybe as an instinctual attempt to hit the delete button in my brain, i.e., "that couldn't possibly have happened, could it?" But it did, and I was left with much to think about.

I went back to bed and tried to go to sleep, but restful slumber wasn't in the hand of cards I'd been dealt that night. It wasn't that I was afraid he'd come back. It was wonderment that such a thing had actually occurred.

After this spectral incident, any time something paranormal happened (or even if it just seemed like it *might* be paranormal), I attributed it to Waya, which is Cherokee for "wolf." The Cherokee tribe is indigenous to our area. Sometimes giving things a name makes them seem more normal.

I never felt threatened by Waya, but after telling Brittany about his visit, she said she'd been seeing a tall man in the kitchen for years that had scared her. I'm not sure that was Waya, though. What she described sounded more like a tall, black shadow.

Interestingly, I would learn a number of years later who the spirit might be and why he was haunting my condo.

Paranormal Tampering with My Work Schedule

I have worked for the same newspaper now for twenty-four years. *The Nashville PRIDE* is a weekly, which means there is a production night—a once a week mad scramble to prepare the paper for the printing press. Often this involves working all day and all night. For fifteen years or so, I worked downtown with everyone else. For the last nine years, I've worked at home even on production night, emailing my copy editing in to the managing editor.

But it wasn't always like that. Back in the day when I worked downtown on production night, we stayed up all night, putting the finishing touches on news stories and getting the layout done.

Many have been the work night/days when I'd meet the bus taking children to school on my way home the next morning.

On one such production night in 2008 as I sat at my desk editing copy, the managing editor, Geraldine Heath, beeped me on the phone saying I had a call from Brittany's husband. It was Kevin, and he was frantic. He said Brittany was "acting out of her head, talking in weird voices, and threatening to hurt herself."

"She doesn't even act like she's Brittany," he exclaimed. "I don't know what's wrong with her. What am I supposed to do? I had to take a knife away from her."

Brittany was pretty strong anyway, but Kevin said that she was displaying strength now that he didn't know she had. He wasn't sure he could control her much longer. He asked if he should call 911 or maybe take her to the emergency room. From past experience, I knew that hospitals and emergency rooms had no lasting help to offer for what was wrong with Brittany.

In all those years of working for the paper, I had never asked to leave before my work was finished on production night. However, I went to the managing editor's office and did just that. Of course, I couldn't tell Geraldine that I was afraid my daughter might be possessed by demons again—so I told her that Brittany was having seizures and her husband didn't know what to do. Geraldine knew that Britt had been under the care of a psychiatrist since she was fifteen and had been in and out of psych ward a number of times. She had known Brittany since she was five years old and genuinely cared about my daughter. I told her that I had seen Britt have these seizures before and knew what to do, asking her if I could leave early and take care of her. Geraldine was an empathetic and gracious person and she was obviously concerned.

"Of course, you can go take care of your baby," Geraldine said. "You tell my girl to get better and that I love her."

I asked to have the rest of my work emailed to me so I could finish it at home.

"You just go take care of my girl and don't worry about this place," she said.

I rushed out to my car and drove the twenty miles to Brittany and Kevin's.

I had been dreading this phone call for many years following the possession. Britt had been subject to severe depression, lack of self-esteem, mood swings, and sometimes near-violent behavior resulting in ongoing psychiatric care. On a few occasions, brief hospitalization resulted. She had difficulties at school, necessitating her mother and I having to go talk with teachers and school officials on numerous occasions.

Before the possession, she was just a happy-go-lucky kid who was generally the life of the party wherever she went. After one of her brief, two-week stays in a juvenile psych ward following a bout of severe depression, she started cutting herself whenever the stress would get too severe to endure. Often she has gone for eight or ten months, even a couple of years, without resorting to the cutting—but regardless of the medications she's been put on, sometimes the cutting just happens. Of all the repercussions from the possession, the cutting is the toughest for me to process. Whenever the cutting occurs, this is when I'd most like to get my hands firmly around the throat of the demon (or whatever body part controls its tether to existence) and squeeze the life out of it.

Finally, after fifteen years of inaccurate diagnoses, we've found a psychiatrist who understands the cause of the problem.

Dr. Elizabeth Baxter has been astute enough to realize that Brittany is suffering from post-traumatic stress disorder caused by the possession when she was fifteen. She has adjusted the treatment accordingly, and the positive results have been little short of amazing.

When I arrived at their townhouse, Kevin met me at my car.

"She's calmed down now," he said, obviously out of breath. "She was talking in some crazy voice, saying things that sounded like they might have been from the Bible, but I really couldn't understand most of it. She was pacing all over the floor, wringing her hands. I tried to get her to just sit down and talk to me, but she threatened to cut herself with a knife if I got any closer."

At that point he had never actually seen her try to harm herself, but he knew her history, had seen the scars, and therefore feared for her safety.

Kevin said she must have grabbed a small butcher knife when she passed through the kitchen, then hid it in her pocket. He was so upset, he wasn't totally sure of what had just happened. He continued to fill me in as we quickly walked up the front porch stairs and went into the house. When he called me at the paper, she was standing in the kitchen with the knife poised to slice her own arm open. He said that when he told Britt (or whoever was inside her manipulating her control levers) that I'd be there soon, Britt passed out and crumpled to the floor. He held her until she came to and then helped her to the sofa.

When I walked in, Brittany was quietly sitting there. She was staring out into space with a wide-eyed, apprehensive expression. I sat down next to her, put my arm around her, and gave her a hug. With that she started crying and speaking so quickly that between the wailing and machine-gun-speed verbiage, I could barely understand her.

"Slow down, slow down," I pleaded. "You've got to stop crying, because I can't understand you. Just tell me what happened. What got this started?"

"I don't know," she blubbered, barely coherent. "We were just talking, and I guess I blacked out. It was like when they [the demons] had me before. They put me in a little room all alone. It was pitch dark, and I couldn't talk. They told me that I was going to die. I was so scared, Daddy. I could hear Kevin talking to me, but I couldn't talk back. Then I heard him say that you were coming. When I came to, Kevin was holding me and we were on the kitchen floor."

Since everything seemed to have pretty much resolved itself by the time I'd arrived, I told Britt and Kevin I'd be heading on home and to call me if there were further problems. Britt was relatively okay, considering, but a bit shaky. She asked if they could follow me back to my house for a cup of coffee. I told her I had to finish my work up on the computer, but they were welcomed to come and hang out while I worked. After we got back to my place and everyone had a cup of coffee and was settled down in the living room, I sat down at my computer nearby them and started back to work.

I could hear Kevin and Brittany chatting about something, but I wasn't paying them any attention. Then everything became quiet.

"Bill. Hey, Bill!" I heard Kevin say in an urgent and much louder voice. He paused. "She's doing it again."

As my eyes looked up from the computer, I saw Brittany begin to slip off the sofa to the floor on her knees. The expression on her face changed from casual to intensely purposeful. Her eyes stared straight ahead like lasers burning a hole in the wall behind me. I bolted up from my desk and strode the twelve feet or so to her, but she continued to stare straight ahead. Not looking at either Kevin or me, she started speaking in a voice that wasn't her own. We could not even vaguely understand her. Kevin and I were both by her side on the floor and holding her within a split second, but she paid neither of us any attention. It was beginning to look like the night was far from over as we listened to her rambling and gibbering on in earnest in some tongue all her own.

I did not recognize her verbalizations as any language with which I was familiar. But my main concern at the time was to avoid another episode of possession, so I didn't waste time ruminating about the accent/language.

I can only say that it sounded like an actual language and not the apparent gibberish you might hear when someone is supposed to be "speaking in tongues." The sounds coming from Brittany had a measured cadence with intonations and genuine expression. Of course, I wish now I had recorded this unidentified language, but at the time I was too preoccupied with Brittany's safety.

I quickly did my best to style my own homemade cleansing based on Laurel's example. I basically gave the same Unity-based sermon used in the hitchhiking demon episode, and it worked. Brittany snapped out of that one rather quickly—but before she had much more than a chance to say hello to us, our Irish friend Spence popped in.

Although Brittany had told Kevin the entire story of the possession, the exorcisms, and the resultant problems—he had never actually seen his wife channel Spence before. I started to introduce him, but Spence good-naturedly cut me short.

"I know who he is, Bill. Don't you remember it's my job to keep an eye on her? I'm always with her," Spence said heartily, making a grand gesture putting Britt's arm around Kevin's shoulder.

The first thing that crossed my mind was, "Why then, if you're always with her, do you let her get into trouble? Why do you let her become so depressed that she cuts herself sometimes?" Though that's what I wanted to say, I didn't. I guess I assumed that guardian angels can't *make* us do anything.

"I can't stay long, you understand," Spence said as we helped Brittany to her feet. "But I'd consider it a kindness if I could take a quick look inside the refrigerator?"

"Sure, help yourself," I replied. "I'd join you, but I have work to do." I actually felt very much reassured now that Spence had made an appearance. I still felt like he'd protect Brittany just as he had on the night of the exorcism.

Brittany/Spence and Kevin went into the kitchen as I sat back down to my computer and went back to work. As I plucked at the keyboard, I could hear Kevin's shy and hesitating responses to Spence's broad prodding and laughter. I could hear the fridge open and close a few times, chairs pulling up to the table, and Kevin trying to tell Spence he really didn't want another helping of whatever they were eating. After about forty-five minutes, I got up and told Spence he'd have to be saying his farewells. Kevin and I both had places to be tomorrow and needed to get some sleep. Time to let Brittany come back. You could tell he was disappointed and would have been happy to keep it up all night—but he somewhat reluctantly told Kevin what a pleasure it was to finally meet him and then bid us adieu. As usual, when Spence left, Britt's head flopped over to the side. Her eyes opened wide and she looked around as if she wasn't sure where she was.

"What did he eat this time?" Brittany asked, shaking her head.

Kevin replied that it was some concoction of corn flakes, sugar, butter, and milk.

"I hate it when he does that," she said. "I'm trying to lose weight!"

Since everything had returned to a more or less equal footing (well, for my family, anyway), I told the kids I needed to finish my work but to call me if anything further happened. They returned home and left me to finish my work. I called Geraldine the next day to make sure they'd received everything okay.

"How's my girl?" she asked.

"Oh, everything's fine now," I replied truthfully. "It was just a mild seizure. The doctor said her new meds might cause that at first," I fibbed. Geraldine was one of my favorite people in the whole world, and I felt comfortable divulging many of our problems to her. She knew a lot of what had happened, but there were certain things I just couldn't share. And I was pretty sure that telling her about Brittany's so-called guardian angel would be stretching the borders of my personal credibility just a bit too far.

From that point forward, I have done all my work for the newspaper at home. Aside from the obvious advantages, this arrangement has also left me available in case my services are needed for any further negative paranormal events.

Angel on Her Shoulder

After Brittany's marriage collapsed in 2010 and she moved back in with me, I discovered that she had developed an alcohol and drug problem during her marriage to Kevin. However, in 2008 I was basically clueless as to any such problem. I mention this because it may help explain why Brittany was at a friend's house drinking around four a.m. with Kevin still at the post office where he worked the night shift. Another factor to consider is that ever since the possession, Britt has been more than just a little apprehensive of being alone—so being married to a guy who had to leave you home alone at night might have been a train wreck waiting to happen.

Britt was at a friend's where she and a group of girls had been having a girls' night out. She was drunk but was in the process of trying to sober up. Her cell phone rang, and Kevin asked her when she was coming home. He had gotten off work a bit early and arrived to find an empty house. (I would learn later it was quite common for him to find Britt absent when he came home around sunup.)

Brittany told Kevin she would be leaving soon and should be home in a few minutes. Her friend only lived six or seven miles away. She got into her 2003 Honda Civic and began the short trek home. There was almost no traffic that time of the morning. Brittany has said that by then she wasn't feeling the effects of the alcohol anymore. I imagine her thoughts were more focused on just how she was going to explain this to Kevin than closely watching the road. The sun was coming up, and weather conditions were dry. Britt's was the only car on the road. She was traveling along a straight stretch, so had no reason to turn the wheel.

Britt said it felt like something took control of the steering wheel from her—a force stronger than she was turning the wheel far to the right. That's the last thing she remembers until she came to, penned in, unable to move, in the wrecked and crumpled Honda. The car had gone off the road and was tipped slightly on its side in the ditch. Then she felt a searing pain shooting from her right ankle. (Coincidentally, she was recuperating from having broken her left ankle a few months earlier after having fallen off a porch—also a result of her drinking problem). Steam was rising from the hood of the car, and not knowing if that was a sign of danger or not, she sensed she should get out of the vehicle. But the door wouldn't open. Totally trapped, she reached into her purse for her phone—but it was nowhere to be found.

Alone, cold, and wretchedly despondent, Brittany sat there in the tilted and crushed Honda and cried. Then she heard the most soothing and reassuring voice.

"It's alright, baby. Everything's going to be okay. I've called the police and they should be here in just a minute." She opened her eyes and saw an African American woman in her early forties standing by the driver's window, reassuring Britt that an ambulance was on the way.

The tall and solidly built woman asked if Britt was hurt anywhere.

"I need to get out, but I'm wedged in and I think I hurt my ankle," Brittany managed to share before a volley of tears overcame her. The woman looked at Britt's feet and noticed the brace she was still wearing on her left ankle. "That one already looks bad, honey."

"No, the other ankle," she said.

But Brittany said the woman was so reassuring and so compassionate, she was immediately put at ease—regardless of the seemingly hopeless situation.

"Is there anyone you need to call?" the woman asked. Brittany said she wanted to call her mother but couldn't find her cell phone. Her benefactor looked into the car and saw the cell phone in the back seat where it had flown during the wreck. The woman reached in, got the phone and handed it to Britt who was shaking so badly she couldn't even dial her mother's number. The kind woman took the phone and keyed in the numbers as Britt dictated. Still asleep, Sheila blearily answered the phone. Brittany exploded into an avalanche of tearful verbiage, and according to Sheila could not be even a little bit understood. Britt's Good Samaritan took the phone and explained to Sheila what had happened, as Britt continued to blubber in the background.

"She told me that Brittany had been in a car wreck but was okay," Sheila said later. "She said she would stay with Brittany until the ambulance arrived." Sheila said the woman handed the phone back to Brittany, and Sheila stayed on the line and listened to her as she cried in the few more minutes it took the police to arrive.

After the police pulled up, Brittany handed the phone to an officer who talked to Sheila, telling her the extent of the accident. He said they had put Britt into an ambulance, and for Sheila to meet them at the hospital a couple of miles away.

Sheila wanted to thank the woman who'd stopped for being such an enormous help, so she asked the officer if she could speak to her again. The officer seemed confused.

"Ma'am, when we got here there was nobody here but your daughter," he said.

"But she stopped and helped," Sheila replied, also confused. "She said she was the one who called the accident in and that she would stay with Brittany until the police and ambulance arrived."

"I don't know what to say, ma'am," the officer said. "Apparently, someone who was just passing by called the wreck in from his or her vehicle. There was no one on the scene when we got here."

Later that day, Sheila called the police station where they verified what the officer had told her. A passerby who had not stopped had called it in. Brittany was alone in the wrecked car when the police arrived.

Sheila was solidly convinced that our benefactor was an angel sent to save Brittany. When Sheila told me about her theory that our benefactor was an angel, I think I just smiled, went along with it, and humored her.

I do know that angels in the Judeo-Christian Bible serve two purposes: (1) as emissaries from God to deliver messages to mankind, and (2) as God's warriors, for example: all the smiting going on in Sodom and Gomorrah. New Age thinkers often equate angels with spirit guides, and that could have very well been her purpose. The facts are that an African American woman rescued Brittany from a serious automobile accident. She talked to Sheila on the phone, and apparently was the one to anonymously call the police. However she disappeared before the police arrived—having said she would remain until the ambulance arrived.

It does seem that such a Good Samaritan would stand there with Brittany until she was out of the car safely and in the ambulance—maybe even stick around long enough to give a report to the police. But there was not a trace of Britt's Good Samaritan.

Frankly, I didn't give this episode much thought one way or the other until several years later when Brittany was looking through some old photographs I had. After my mom died, I was left to go through boxes upon boxes of loose photos.

One day Brittany came over, as I was sorting through photos, bent over me and said, "That's my angel."

"What? Angel, what angel?" I asked, totally out of sync with her thought processes of the moment.

"When I had the wreck and broke my other ankle," she said excitedly. "That's the angel who waited with me till the police came."

She was talking about a small group of pictures I had of our housekeeper/nanny Maggie from the fifties and sixties. Maggie was my favorite person when I was growing up. She wasn't just a housekeeper to me. She was a playmate, a confidante, and a best friend—always there with a wise laugh to solve the biggest problems perplexing a little kid. After my father died, when I was sixteen, my mom had to let Maggie go. We just didn't have the money to pay her. But for eleven years, she was probably the single most important person in my life.

Britt was adamant about Maggie being the actual angel who had saved her when she totaled her Honda. How could she be so sure? She had only met Maggie once when she was eleven or twelve when I took McCartney and her to visit Maggie at her home in Springfield, Tennessee, and Maggie passed away a few years later. Did Britt's subconscious somehow remember Maggie's face and superimpose it on an imaginary entity her mind created as she lay semiconscious after the wreck? The Maggie Britt met was an elderly woman. The angel was middle-aged and about the same age as the Maggie in the photos I had. Britt had never seen those photos before.

Unless we're all crazy, Brittany's angel sure appears to be the spirit of Maggie manifesting the way she would have looked in early middle age. I don't believe that when good people die they become angels; angels are separate entities created by God for totally different purposes. But I can accept the premise that Maggie's spirit is one of Britt's guides.

I also can't shake the notion that the accident might have been caused by negative entities still lingering in Britt's psyche. She still asserts that just before the accident, she lost control of the car. The wheel was pulled hard in the opposite direction she was trying to steer. Would it be that far-fetched to think that a demonic entity might attempt murder by automobile?

The Teleporting Wheelchair

My mother, "Mima" to the kids, was in remarkably good shape for her age when most of these things were going on. After Brittany got married in 2005, Mima spent the majority of her time at her apartment. She did have a scare with a case of non-Hodgkin's lymphoma. The doctor felt like she was too old for chemotherapy; however, after a round of radiation treatments, she was declared to be in remission and cancer-free. She didn't let any of this slow her down much. She still drove and even took herself to most of her radiation treatments.

But during the winter of her eighty-fifth year, she came down with pneumonia. It took her down fast and hard. At first, she just thought she had a cold. But after a week in bed, it was apparent more was going on. I'd been trying to get her to go to the doctor since she first got sick, but she didn't like doctors. She didn't trust them and thought they charged too much. She was determined to stick it out and get better on her own. But she kept getting worse, so one day I just announced that it was time to go to the doctor. She weakly protested, but by then was not strong enough to resist much.

She stayed almost a month in the hospital, and then had to go to a nursing home to get physical therapy. After lying in bed so long, her legs didn't want to hold her up anymore. After another month of physical therapy, she finally got to where she could walk with a walker for brief distances—but had to carry around an oxygen tank wherever she went.

When she left the nursing/rehab center, I took her back to her apartment to live. She could never walk without the walker or drive her car again. Although she would have liked to return home with me, I couldn't take her back to my condo. There was simply no way we could get her and the walker up the steep steps to my front door—let alone up and down the stairs to get to a bedroom or take a shower.

Mima slowly got better and shed that cumbersome oxygen tank after several more months. But the walker forced her to live full time in her apartment from then on. Since she couldn't drive, once a week I'd go fetch her groceries, and I took her to her doctor once a month. For these excursions, we got a folding wheelchair.

I'd stop in and have dinner with her every week or two. She'd make spaghetti for me or maybe falafels, and then we'd sit and talk about current events. After a couple more years, she could no longer cook, so I'd bring dinner.

Then in September of 2010, around ten p.m., she fell out of her wheelchair and couldn't get up. She was too weak to crawl to the phone and didn't have a cell phone. Luckily, she lived in a retirement center and the other residents were always checking up on each other. Someone in the hallway heard Mima calling for help and rescued her. An ambulance arrived and took her to the hospital.

It was production night at the newspaper, and I was working. I had a cell phone and she had the number, but she didn't have anyone call. I guess Mima knew I'd be busy and didn't want to bother me. After we'd finished around dawn, I was so tired I didn't even check the messages on my machine (when I'm working I turn the ringer off). When I got up around noon, I discovered a message from St. Thomas Hospital telling me my mother had fallen and was a patient there. She was stable, but I should call. I called the hospital, got her room number, and rushed down there.

She was exhausted and heavily sedated. I chastised her for not calling me, but that was a little like giving a speech to the mailbox. The doctors were very concerned with her general weakness and particularly the weakness in her legs. Plus, there was significant pain in her legs. During the next few days, they ran many tests. They determined her cancer had come back. It was centered in her legs and spreading rapidly. I asked what treatments were available and how the prognosis looked. The very kind and compassionate oncologist just said they were going to make her as comfortable as possible, but she probably only had another month or so to live. She was put under hospice care, and everyone prepared for the worst.

However, Mima was a tough old gal and started feeling better. After a month in the hospital, her doctor recommended transferring her to a nursing facility. We moved her to a nursing home about eight miles from my home. Sheila, Brittany, and I would go see her every evening. Although she'd seemed to be getting stronger, after a couple more weeks the improvements started to reverse. The pain was getting much worse, but thank God for morphine.

Mima died on November 7, 2010, at the age of eight-nine, two months shy of turning ninety.

We donated a lot of Mima's things to Goodwill, but I thought it would be a nice gesture to give her wheelchair to the Presbyterian church Sheila had been attending for the past few years. I called the minister, who was eager receive the donation. He said they had several church members who could benefit from its use.

When I loaded the wheelchair into my car, I realized one of the footrests was missing. I went back in and looked in the closet where it had been stored. The footrest wasn't anywhere in sight, and I'd already made an appointment with the church secretary to meet her and deliver the wheelchair. I decided to go ahead and take it to the church and come back and find the footrest later.

I spent the rest of that day and the next ransacking the house looking for that footrest. I looked under everything, in every closet and drawer. It was nowhere to be found. I thought that maybe it had gotten lost in the move or fallen off the moving truck. But then I remembered putting the entire device back together once I got home and sitting in it as I went through some of her things. Both footrests had made the trip. It had to be there somewhere.

I continued to look for it in my spare time throughout the following week. Nothing. It seemed to simply have vanished into thin air. There aren't that many places it could have hidden in my one-thousand-square-foot condo, and I covered those thousand square feet with a fine-toothed comb. It wasn't there.

During this time, I was living alone. There was no one else in the house who could have moved it. I even cast accusing looks at the cats, but the footrest was made mostly of steel and probably weighed twelve to fifteen pounds. I've never seen a cat that could bat around twelve to fifteen pounds of steel. I even considered a group effort, with the five of them pooling their furry resources. But the theory of a grand feline group heist didn't make sense. It had disappeared into the ether.

Defeated, I called the pastor and told him I couldn't find the footrest and expressed my deepest apologies. He was very gracious about it and said he was sure the church could buy a replacement.

The next morning, I got up and went downstairs to get my first cup of coffee. The front door is directly in front of the bottom of the staircase. There's a very small foyer, and then you turn left to go into the living room. Sitting in front of the door was the footrest. How did it get there? Who or what put it there? There was no one who could have moved it from wherever it had been hiding and put it out there in plain view. It couldn't have been there the whole time. Someone would have tripped over it coming in or out of the door.

Did some spirit teleport it there to help me out? Did Waya, the Native American spirit, take pity on me after seeing me tear the house apart looking for the footrest and put it there? Did Mima's spirit put it there, so it could be reunited with the rest of her wheelchair? I guess this little episode will just have to remain a mystery. Regardless, I called the minister and told him I'd found the missing footrest and took it to the church the next day.

Chapter 14
Life Goes On

Brittany and Kevin got divorced after five years of marriage, not long after Mima died. He neglected her due to a preoccupation with video games, and she reacted with infidelity. Both share responsibility. Kevin kept the house, and Brittany moved back in with me in December of 2010.

I thought having Britt move back in at twenty-five would be like having a roommate, but let's just say those were tumultuous times.

For the first couple of years, there seemed to be a revolving door of boyfriends coming and going—that I could adjust to. But I also discovered that while Britt had been married, she'd developed a drug and alcohol problem—mostly alcohol, but marijuana and hydrocodone also entered into it.

From the perspective of the paranormal, I feel compelled to discuss Brittany's drug and alcohol problem to some extent—because the abuse of drugs and alcohol can seriously alter the psychic reception of those with that gift. The doctors have told us that alcohol could be a deadly mixture with the prescription drugs she was already taking to alleviate the depression and anxiety caused by her PTSD. She has been in and out of Alcoholics Anonymous, and at times it seemed to work. There were a couple of periods of sobriety (lasting two to ten months), but for the most part the disease of alcoholism seemed to be winning. However, as I write this, she is doing quite well and has been sober for some time.

I believe in miracles, and I firmly believe God has something in mind for Brittany that she can't find in mood-altering drugs or alcohol.

A Friend Indeed

After Brittany moved back in with me, she became friends with my next-door neighbor Tracy—a single mom with two teenaged kids. Tracy was thirteen years older than Britt, but they quickly became great pals—or more like big sister/little sister. Tracy knew about Britt's experiences with the paranormal and was totally sympathetic, having had more than a few experiences in her own time. In fact, she and her children claimed to have seen spirits in their condo. Tracy considered herself Pagan and a seeker of ultimate truth just as Brittany did.

Tracy was by far the best next-door neighbor I've ever had. She would do anything in the world for you, and because of that, you wanted to return the favor. We'd loan each other things like in a fifties sitcom. If her car wouldn't start, I'd help her get it started. She was a computer genius, so if Britt's computer went down, Tracy could fix it. I gave her much of my mom's old furniture when Mima died.

Brittany looked up to Tracy like a big sister and would take her good advice, even when the same advice from her mother and me usually fell on deaf ears. Tracy talked her out of several wild adventures that would have caused heartache for everyone involved, not just herself. She even helped Brittany get a good job working for the supermarket where Tracy had worked for a number of years.

At one point in 2014 when Britt and I were having a rough go of it due primarily to her problems with alcohol, Tracy offered to let Britt move in with her as long as she paid very modest rent and *did not* drink alcohol. That arrangement didn't last, though. Brittany kept sneaking beer in, and after a couple of weeks, Tracy kicked her out. However, their friendship endured. Britt said she understood why Tracy had to send her back to live with me. There were rules, and she had broken them.

I had the greatest admiration for Tracy, because she worked two or three low-paying jobs at a time to support her kids and put them through school—all the while attending junior college to learn computer technology.

But Tracy was not in the best health. She suffered from sickle cell anemia, fibromyalgia, and a thyroid disorder. Once, she described to me all the medications they had her on. I wondered at the time if she should be mixing all those drugs together.

It was New Year's Eve of 2014, and Tracy hadn't shown up for a party where her boyfriend had expected to meet her. But he just figured she had found something better to do, so didn't think much else about it. He called her later that night but got no answer. Tracy's friend Carol Humphrey (owner of Mystical Heart New Age Book Store) called Tracy several times during New Year's Day but also never got an answer. So that evening around seven p.m., Carol came and rang Tracy's doorbell. There was no reply, but Tracy's car was in her designated space out front.

Carol and Tracy had keys to each other's homes in case of emergencies, but Carol came and got Brittany before she went in. They called Tracy but were answered only with silence. All the lights in the condo were on. Carol went upstairs to check Tracy's bedroom, while Britt said she'd check in the kitchen. Britt noticed the front burner to the stove was on with a half-full milk bottle precariously close by. Then her eyes shifted to the floor where she saw Tracy's lifeless body.

Britt and Carol called 911 then came back to my condo. They were both very upset, but Britt was almost hysterical. I tried to console her, saying maybe the paramedics could revive Tracy and not to give up. But they said they were sure she was not breathing and was turning a bluish color.

By this time, both Tracy's kids had left home and were living elsewhere. But Dillon and Kristin Newell (the children of Tracy and her first husband), along with several carloads of their friends, were quick to come home when Brittany called them with the bad news. For the rest of the evening, my little condo was meeting place central for paramedics and policemen investigating the scene and family and friends coming to pay their respects. Tracy was forty-two years old when she had her fatal heart attack—a truly sad fate for one with such a big heart.

When Tracy died that cold January 1, Brittany had just completed ten months of sobriety. She seemed on the verge of getting her life back together. I was so proud of her, I had sent out Christmas cards to family and friends with a little note attached bragging about how well I thought she had adjusted. Her dramatic recuperation, spiritually and emotionally, was due in no small part to Tracy's positive influence. However, finding Tracy dead on her kitchen floor on New Year's Day just seemed to cause Brittany to go into a tailspin. It wasn't long before she was drinking again and getting involved with old friends that seemed to have a penchant for getting themselves and her into trouble.

After Tracy died, Brittany started having nightmares again—particularly about finding Tracy's body (the autopsy said she had probably been dead for twelve hours or so when Britt found her), but also about her possession that had happened almost exactly fourteen years earlier.

Britt's nightmares are always related in some way to the possession. They cause her to remember it, and that memory causes bouts of PTSD, which is in turn caused by the possession. Then the PTSD causes her destructive behavior. It's a vicious circle of negativity.

Brittany wrote the following narrative in the spring of 2014, before Tracy died, and during her longest period of sobriety up to that date:

Britt's Narrative about Her Sobriety

To be honest, it's followed me to this very day [the demonic entity]. It whispers that I'm nothing and nobody will ever love me— that my parents hate me, etc. I fight them on a daily basis, and normally I win. I was never diagnosed by any psychiatrist or psychotherapist with schizophrenia or for having any hallucinations.

This shit is real; this is my life. I can't do anything without hearing and seeing all the evil in this world.

I used drugs and alcohol to cope with this bitter situation, but it made it worse. I am happy to say for the first time in a long time, I'm without drugs and alcohol.

But after finding Tracy's lifeless body, she did go back to drinking. The nightmares led to more drinking and drugs, which led to widespread association with unsavory characters, which eventually led to involvement with law enforcement. During the seven years she lived back with me, Britt was on probation twice—both times resulting from domestic disputes with boyfriends that caused physical fights.

In fact, trouble has followed Brittany around like a hungry, stray cat since the possession in 2001. Besides her discipline problems in high school, her troublesome marriage to Kevin, and the seemingly never-ending trail of bad boy relationships, she has totaled more cars than anyone I have ever known—three. Once she even charged her car into a house, making the six o'clock news on local TV. Her big Impala, which I'd picked because cops drive them, looked like a sardine can a T-Rex stepped on; a wall nearly collapsed on the house.

But she escaped all accidents unharmed, so perhaps Maggie was also on hand during her two later serious accidents. No physical sightings of an angel after those last crashes, but you can't help but wonder if God has something important planned for Brittany.

He Takes Off His Hat to No Man

One of the most recent boyfriends was a young man named Rick. When Brittany started dating him, Rick had a full-time job in the cafeteria of a nursing home near our condo. He was living with his mother nearby. He seemed like a nice guy, a good speaker, and very intelligent. Britt told me he not only had a literary blog he wrote on the internet, but also sporadically published a small magazine reviewing movies when he could afford to put it out. I genuinely liked him at first.

After they'd been an item for a month or so, Rick had an argument with his stepfather and he kicked Rick out of the house. He didn't have enough money saved up for all the deposits on his own apartment yet, so he was basically homeless. Britt begged and pleaded for me to let him stay with us for just a few days till he could get his own place. Old softie that I am, I folded and told them he could stay a couple of days till he could find a permanent home. Well, a couple of days turned into a couple of weeks and still no progress on finding a home for Rick. But it wasn't really all that bad an arrangement. Although he wasn't paying me rent, every day he would bring home hot food that the nursing home had left over—so I guess that was compensation of a sort.

But then Rick got into an argument with his boss for refusing to remove his baseball hat inside the building and lost his job. He spent the next two weeks unemployed but going on numerous interviews. Finally, he landed two part-time jobs at two different restaurants—with a combined income of less than he had made at the nursing home.

But the better I got to know Rick, the more erratic he seemed. I observed that he was more than a little short tempered with Brittany, but I tried to stay out of their ups and downs. He was also extremely opinionated about politics, with political inclinations the opposite of my own. If I sensed the conversation headed down a political lane, I tried to change the subject. Mood swings were also just a part of the package.

I learned that Rick had been under the care of a psychiatrist for a number of years. He was supposed to be taking several prescriptions, but because of his dire financial straits could no longer afford the office visits needed to get his prescriptions.

Finally, after two months of living in my home for free, I confronted Rick about seeking more gainful employment so he could get his own place. I didn't lose my temper or criticize him in any way. His part-time jobs proved he was at least trying. But he seemed perfectly content working part-time and wasn't seriously looking for anything else. I tried to point out to Rick that he was going to have to be the breadwinner in his relationship with Brittany. She had no job and her work history left much to be desired. I told him he couldn't expect her to be their major source of income. I attempted to broach these realities as I would with a friend and as delicately as possible. However he reacted very negatively, blew up like a raging volcano, and cursed me like I've never been cursed by anyone before or since. He went berserk, screaming and yelling at the top of his lungs. I then firmly told Rick to pack his things and get out of my house. He stormed upstairs and shared his rage with Brittany.

I heard them arguing, making up, and then arguing again. At one point I did hear Brittany tell Rick he shouldn't have spoken to me the way he did. But after all was said and done, she took his side and moved out with him.

This episode left me more than a little depressed, but I took some consolation from reading my old Bible, front to back, cover to cover, like you'd read a novel. I'd always told myself I'd do this someday, and now seemed like a good time. I had always wanted to see what exactly was in there, and not just take some priest, minister, or rabbi's word for it. I also started wearing a little cross given to me by the Greek Orthodox priest I'd talked to about performing an exorcism on Brittany years before. Father Nicholas gave it to me in my darkest hour, but I put it in a drawer where it languished for fourteen years. I found it and wear it to this day.

The newly liberated couple found a room to rent in a nearby home owned by a friend of Rick's. I saw very little of either of them for several months. I was seriously concerned, but parents of adult children often have to step aside and let the universe operate on autopilot. I had to believe there was a higher power manning the controls.

Chapter 15
The Return

One evening in 2015, I was working at home. Brittany called me about six p.m. My answering machine is very old-school, set up so I can hear who is leaving a message and I don't have to take calls I'm not interested in. But I quickly picked up when I heard the desperation in her voice. She was frantic, crying, and I couldn't understand what she was saying. I tried to get her to slow down.

"Daddy, they're back," she said. "It's happening all over again."

I knew in my heart what she meant, but I asked anyway, "Who's back? What are you talking about?"

Then there was more uncontrollable sobbing.

"Brittany, slow down; I can't understand you."

She took a deep breath and continued, "Just like fifteen years ago. I hear all these voices in my head, and I can't block them out. They're telling me to hurt myself, to kill myself. They're saying I'm no good; I'm worthless; I'll never be anything—to kill myself and come with them. Please, help me. I don't know what to do."

My first thought was to determine if she was alone. I didn't know if Rick had gotten home from work by then or not. They lived about four miles from me.

"Is Rick there, or are you by yourself?" I asked.

"Rick's here. He doesn't know what to do. He just says I have multiple personalities. I've been talking in different voices, but I don't remember it. I was sitting on the side of the bed, and he said I started talking in some language he didn't recognize. He said it wasn't Latin, but he didn't know what it was. Then he said I just sort of passed out and fell off the bed. The only thing I remember is waking up on the floor."

Well, I knew it wouldn't do me any good to talk to Rick. Aside from our personal differences, I also knew that he had no spiritual beliefs whatsoever. As far as I knew, he was either agnostic or completely atheist—and he didn't have room for any sort of paranormal philosophies in his own personal belief system. Back when we were still getting along, we had been having a friendly discussion about the plausibility of metaphysics in the universe. I told him about Brittany's experiences with possession and channeling when she was fifteen. He'd been exposed to the notion that she had paranormal encounters, but he'd never actually been involved in an episode. I didn't know if he'd be a help or a hindrance.

"Daddy, help me. I don't know what to do," she pleaded.

"Okay, we're going to take care of this," I assured her. "Just try to be calm." I was totally rattled by this but knew the first order of business was to settle Brittany down.

I told Britt that I'd been reading about Jewish mysticism and had learned that there are Jewish exorcists. I'd learned that in the book of Psalms, there are a number of passages that are used to cast out demons in exorcisms performed by rabbis. I had reread the entire Book of Psalms, paying particular attention to Psalms 10, 20, 90, 91, and 127.

I knew I needed to get to Brittany as soon as I could, but I had one personal physical complication preventing me from hopping into my car and rushing to her house. My cataracts didn't permit me to drive at night. Since it was mid-January, it was already dark by the time she called. That wouldn't have been safe for me or anyone else on the road.

"Let me call your mom and see if she'll come pick me up," I said. "Everything's going to be all right. I'll call you back in just a minute."

I called Sheila and only got her voice mail. I told her we had a situation with Brittany—the thing we'd all dreaded most for the last fifteen years had happened again. It looked like whatever had possessed her as a teenager had returned. While I waited for Sheila to return my call, I went upstairs and pulled out the Bible I'd been reading for my Psalms research.

I called Brittany back and was discouraged to hear the voice of someone I didn't even remotely recognize. A very faint female voice answered the phone. Based on past experience, I was fairly certain I was speaking with some channeled entity. Whether good or bad, I didn't know.

"Yes?" said Britt/the entity, no longer sounding distressed at all.

"Brittany? Is that you?"

"Yes, it is." The voice was Brittany's, but the intonations were totally off from her usual pattern.

"You don't sound like Brittany."

"Who do I sound like?" it calmly asked. There was just a hint of mockery in her tone.

"I really don't know, but you don't sound like my daughter."

"Well, what does your daughter sound like?" it asked. Frankly, the voice didn't really sound menacing or evil. It just wasn't Britt.

"Brittany, look, I'm waiting for your mother to call me back. Meanwhile, I want you to listen to these passages from Psalms."

After I'd read about three sentences from the first passage, I heard a click. She'd hung up on me. I wasn't surprised; I hadn't really expected a possessing entity to attentively listen while I read off words that would cast it out. I really didn't know what else to do; I was stalling.

Sheila called me back within a couple of minutes. I filled her in on my calls with Britt, and she said she would come and get me. As I waited, I held the Bible and prayed. I was shaking. I did not in any way feel qualified for the task that fate had assigned me. I had assisted Laurel in Brittany's original exorcism, even talked down Brittany's demons a few times on my own. But this somehow felt different. I had long thought that the exorcism when she was a teen may not have been sufficient—maybe something had been left in there all these years. Now it was going to be on my shoulders to do the job right, and I frankly did not feel qualified. After a few minutes, the phone rang again. It was Brittany in that same otherworldly, detached voice.

"Bill?" it asked.

"Uh, yes. Who is this?"

"It doesn't matter who I am," it assured me. The voice didn't sound threatening or evil, just rather indifferent.

"Well, it matters to me if you're inhabiting my daughter."

"But everything is okay now," it said. "I just wanted to let you know there's no need for you to come over. We're fine. We're going to watch a movie now." I assumed that "we" was Brittany, Rick, and whomever I was talking to.

"I need to know who I'm talking to. What's your name?" I asked.

The entity replied with "Lola" or something like that. I really couldn't understand it. I asked it to repeat itself, but I never could quite get the name.

"Let me talk to Brittany," I demanded.

"There's no need for that," it replied. "We're all fine. We're going to watch a movie."

For a split second, I strangely wondered what kind of film demons or wannabe demons like. I had to shake my head to come out of that disconnected, abstract thought, and couldn't help but wonder if the entity had actually placed it in my head just to show me it could.

"Well, I don't think Brittany is fine," I replied, struggling to reconnect with reality. "Look, Brittany, now listen: I talked to your mom, and she's coming to get me. We'll be over there is a few minutes."

"I told you that you don't need to come over here," it said.

"Okay, well you let me decide that. Meanwhile ..." I picked up where I'd left off reading from Psalms 10. Again, I got through a few sentences and was hung up on.

While I waited for Sheila to come after me, I thumbed through the verses in Psalms I'd be reading soon. I continued to tremble and feel inadequate for the task before me.

Within a few minutes, Sheila had arrived and we headed over to Brittany's. During the fifteen-minute trip, Sheila talked but I honestly don't remember much of what she said. Somehow I instinctively knew I needed to keep my mind essentially blank in order to steel myself for what was coming. If there's such a thing as an extremely nervous meditative state, then maybe I was in it. I was still gently trembling and blankly staring out into the darkness. Perhaps the cataracts were the only link I had anchoring me to the real world. I had to shield my eye from the glare of the headlights meeting our car every few seconds, and that may have been the thing that kept me attached to physical reality.

We did briefly discuss whether it would be better to conduct the exorcism we were about to do at Brittany's home or go back to one of our houses. We concluded that we should do whatever Britt was most comfortable with.

When we pulled up into the parking lot behind Brittany and Rick's tiny apartment, Britt came out to meet us. I didn't know what to expect. Would she still be talking in that odd, detached voice she'd used on the phone? Or could we expect something worse, something like the demonic entity it had taken several people to hold down when she was fifteen and sixteen? But the Brittany personality appeared to be back in charge. When I got out of the car, she hugged me and then went over and hugged her mother. She told us how scared she was but was so glad we were there. With very few words, we followed Britt back into the house and up the stairs to the room she and Rick were renting from his friend.

I asked her to tell me what had been happening, and she recounted the things she'd told me on the phone the first time she called (before the two calls from Lola). Rick was shy and reluctant to say much at first, since he hadn't been on speaking terms with

Sheila or me for several months. But he loosened up a bit after a few minutes, concurring with what Brittany said about how she had been speaking in some language he didn't recognize—and then she'd passed out while sitting on the bed and fallen onto the floor. He said he'd never seen anything like the way she'd been acting.

I listened to everyone talk but didn't say much myself. I was still in that zone that seemed to separate me from everything that was going on around me. I held the Bible on my lap as I sat on the side of their bed. My heart was racing, and I knew I was about to go somewhere I'd never been before, but I oddly also felt at peace. It's not that I suddenly felt like I knew what I was doing. I didn't. But I felt strangely calm, maybe like that proverbial calm before the storm.

The only furniture in their bedroom consisted of the bed, several bookshelves, and an easy chair. Sheila sat in the chair; Rick was still standing; I sat on the side of the bed; and Brittany sat at the foot of the bed.

Brittany commented that her head was really hurting and she was feeling dizzy. She started to sway and then fell lifelessly back in the bed. None of this particularly alarmed me since we'd been through similar episodes with the very first possession and afterward, when she did her channeling. However, it had been a number of years since I'd seen her go through this, so I didn't take it lightly. I scooted over next to her and touched her cheek. She seemed asleep at first, but then after a couple of seconds, her eyes slowly opened. There's very little difference between possession and channeling during the waking phase with Brittany. You may never know who's going to be there when she opens her eyes, but it only takes half a second to know it's not her.

She had a big grin on her face and a twinkle in her eye, so I knew almost without her speaking that this was Spence. I was reassured, because Laurel had considered Spence one of the good guys.

With his lilting Irish brogue, Spence greeted everyone, and told us it looked like there was another fight coming. He said he'd dropped by to keep an eye on her but wouldn't be able to stay long. He's so contagiously good natured, you almost forget that when Spence comes around, there are usually metaphysical dark clouds on the horizon.

Spence carried on friendly banter with Sheila and me for maybe ten minutes, then said, "Oh, dear," and Brittany's expression changed to total surprise. Her eyes got bigger, and she fell backward onto the bed with a bounce. I leaned over her, and she appeared to have gone to sleep. Since the presence of Spence so often precluded communication from other entities, both good and bad, I fully expected the emergence of something more than unpleasant sitting back up from the bed—perhaps the entity I had spoken with on the phone an hour earlier. But when her eyes opened, the only one looking out was obviously Brittany. As she sat up, she surveyed the room and said simply, "Well, he hasn't been around in a long time."

Since all this started years ago, Britt has maintained that whenever she channels Spence, she has given him full permission to take over.

"He does the talking and calls the shots, but he always asks my permission and always tells me I can step in at any time and correct what he's said or take the control back any time I want," she has explained.

She expressed the need to go to the bathroom after this, so she and Sheila headed down the hall, leaving Rick and me in the room.

That was a bit awkward, since we hadn't seen or spoken with each other for over two months. After a few seconds, I asked him for a piece of paper I could tear up so I could mark the places of the five different psalms I'd be using. He readily complied, and about the time I got that accomplished, the ladies returned.

"So what do you want to do?" Sheila asked.

"I'd like to go back to Mom's house," she said.

We drove to Sheila's townhouse with Brittany and Rick in the backseat and me in the front passenger's seat with the Bible in my lap. Once inside, Brittany and Rick sat at the dining room table; Sheila stood nearby; and I stood by Brittany while holding the Bible.

Sheila has a bookcase near the dining room for her angel figurine collection. But after settling in, Britt remarked: "I don't like those angels. They make me uncomfortable. They're ugly." At that point, she was still very much herself—but oddly expressing disdain for angels, many of which she had given her mother herself over the years.

"And I don't like that ring," she continued, pointing to a hematite ring I was wearing that she'd given me a few weeks before as a Christmas present. She'd bought it in a metaphysical bookstore. Hematite is supposed to have protective properties guarding one from negative spirits.

"And I really don't like that," she said pointing to the Bible. "I don't know why I feel this way. I bought some of those angels and the ring." She didn't have any sort of vacant look on her face—or that weird gleam in her eyes I'd seen years before indicating that someone else was in there.

"Well, I guess we'd better get started then," I said.

I opened the Bible and started reading from one of the first passages I'd marked. After I'd read three or four sentences, Brittany got up and made a quick beeline for the kitchen. I also popped up but continued reading from Psalms. Carrying a large, hardbound, four-pound, study-sized Bible and trying to out-pace a demonically motivated twenty-nine-year-old was a tall order for a sixty-four-year-old man—but I was hoping to protect her from the knives in the kitchen. I managed to get to the drawer first and block Brittany's efforts without losing my place or dropping the book.

"This is over," she said. "You need to get away from me, old man. You can't stop me."

Then she reached for the doorknob leading into the laundry room. I didn't know if there was anything in there she could hurt herself with, but I thought it best to get her stabilized in order for me to continue. With one hand holding the Bible, I wrapped the other around her shoulders. As we stood there semi-entwined, she refused to be still and started making a low growling sound, adding an unwanted, eerie sound effect to a procedure I had hoped would be more peaceful—and stationary. My attempts to restrain her and read at the same time were failing, and before long I had dropped the Bible on the kitchen counter. I had prevented her from opening the knife drawer, but now it was all I could do to keep her from taking off into the laundry room.

Something told me that the demonic entity knew, using Brittany's knowledge of her mother's house, there was something in the laundry room that could be used to hurt Britt (or maybe us), so it was important to keep her out. But she pushed me away and I fell back a step. Luckily Sheila had followed us into the kitchen, and she restrained Brittany while I picked up the Bible and resumed reading from Psalms 91:

"You will not fear the terror of the night; nor the arrow that flies by day; nor the pestilence that stalks in the darkness; nor the plague that destroys at midday. A thousand may fall at your side, ten thousand at your right hand, but it will not come near you."

As I read, the growling continued, and within a moment, Sheila and I both had been pulled back to the floor. In a reflexive movement to keep from losing my place, I rolled to the side. Then Brittany's demon wrapped her legs around one of her mother's legs, and we heard a crunching sound and a shrieking wail from Sheila. Whoever was possessing Brittany took the opportunity to jump up and bolt into the laundry room, slamming the door.

"Rick, stop her," Sheila yelled.

Looking up, I could see Rick's feet rush past me. He and Brittany fought for control of the louvered door, with it opening and slamming shut a number of times before he finally forced his way inside. The door banged shut a final time with both of them in there. We couldn't see what was going on, but we could hear the growling and the scuffling. After a few seconds, we could hear a resounding thud where they'd both lurched to the floor. Then came a hollow, metallic thumping as they'd slammed up against the washing machine.

Although I was no longer able to see Brittany, I knew she could still hear me, and the whole point of the exorcism was to have the entity confronted with the words of God. I continued reading even as Brittany/the entity kicked the louvered slats out of the door. The raging growl crescendoed into a frenzied wail as Sheila managed to open the door, through her own pain, wide enough for Rick to force his possessed girlfriend back out into the kitchen.

"Your hand will lay hold on your enemies; your right hand will seize your foes. At the time of your appearing, you will make them like a fiery furnace. In his wrath the Lord will swallow them up, and his fire will consume them," I read from Psalms 21. As the commotion and growling got louder, so did my volume. Filling a theatre with the resonance of my voice had been good training.

Rick continued to hold the entity tight as we stood in the kitchen and I read from Psalms. Brittany flailed in all directions at first, but he subdued her and held her arms tight.

During the whole ordeal, I was always careful to constantly re-assure the entity that God loved it and that it needed to return to the light from which it had originally come—that there would be no punishment upon its return to God, only a welcoming love and rejoicing at the reunification.

The Jewish mystic's approach to exorcism is very similar to the methods used by Laurel. They do not condemn the possessing entity to burn in never ending hell for its transgressions. There is an emphasis on forgiveness for the entity's misunderstanding of God's truth and the natural order of the universe. This, to me, seems more in line with a God emanating from pure love.

The growling and wailing kept up for a couple more minutes, but it seemed that my promises of God's understanding and forgiveness were making an impact. Then the growling stopped. The expression on Brittany's face changed from anger and rage to an intense interest and finally to understanding and acceptance. As I stood next to Brittany and Rick reading from Psalms, Brittany suddenly went limp. Then her head flopped over to the side as if she'd lost consciousness. Rick and Sheila got her back into a chair at the table. Her eyes opened, and she looked up at us as if she hadn't seen us for hours.

"What happened?" she asked. "Oh, my leg is killing me!" Brittany started to sit up but lay quickly back down. "Oh, my God! Everything hurts!" She complained about pain in her legs and back—predictable for a physical body only recently wrestled to the floor several times.

Brittany's leg was bruised, and she could barely stand. The violent melee also took its toll on Sheila, as her leg was swollen and bruised. Luckily, no one had broken anything.

Even though relative tranquility had returned and Brittany had resumed her own personality, I thought it might be a good idea to read more from the Psalms just to see what kind of effect they'd have on her. After all, she had seemed fine just before the exorcism—but had complained that she was uncomfortable with the angels, the hematite ring and the Bible. I started by asking her if she'd like to hear a bit more before we called an end to the evening.

"Yes, I would, please," she replied.

I finished with the following from Psalms 91: "If you make the most High your dwelling—even the Lord, who is my refuge—then no harm will befall you, no disaster will come near your tent. For he will command his angels concerning you to guard you in all your ways; they will lift you up in their hands ..." Then I skipped down to: "'Because he loves me,' says the Lord, 'I will rescue him; I will be with him in trouble, I will deliver him and honor him. With long life will I satisfy him and show him my salvation.'"

Things seemed to have gone exceptionally well, especially considering my apprehensions beforehand. During the procedure, part of me felt like I was totally winging it, while the other part was absolutely convinced that God would hear our prayers and guarantee a positive outcome. Of course, Brittany wasn't acting cheerful or upbeat after what she'd just gone through, but she was at least relaxed and peaceful.

We were all drained and relieved that it was over. It was about midnight and general fatigue had replaced our original anxiety about facing down an evil entity. We took Britt and Rick back to their place, and then Sheila dropped me off.

As soon as I walked in the door, I could hear Brittany's voice on the answering machine. She was already calling me back. Fearing the worst, I rushed to the phone and picked up.

"Daddy, all the voices in my head! I can't get them to stop," Brittany said. "Who are all these people? Everyone is talking at once. I can't understand what they all want!"

As soon as she and Rick had gotten back inside and tried to wind down, she suddenly started getting psychic voicemails inside her head. She wasn't seeing ghosts, but it sounded like she was hearing them from every direction. I told Britt that it seemed to me that once the demon was chased off, her psyche had become a clear channel for ghosts with messages they thought they needed to get to the living.

I told her that she needed to tell them all they did not have permission to come in and take over. If she wanted to help them, then she could in her own good time. But for tonight, she was tired and needed to rest. I explained that she had to put up barriers to protect herself.

She hasn't complained again about multiple spirits trying to take over her head since then, so I assume my explanation worked.

Obviously the entity we encountered that night meant Brittany harm. Was it a demon or fallen angel loyal only to Satan? What exactly was it?

Laurel had a theory that there are intrinsically evil human spirits she called "wraiths" that have been dead so long and are so very wicked that they've convinced themselves they are actually demonic entities rather than human. But wraiths, regardless of their self-delusion, are still just human. No matter where such entities are from, what exactly they are, or why they want to possess the bodies of humans—they do not belong here. They are infringing on our reality.

Whatever the entity we dealt with that night was, demon or wraith, it appeared to be gone. I hope that it was somehow reunited with God, no matter what it was.

Again, I asked Brittany if she could write down her impression of being possessed by another entity. Her narrative follows:

Brittany's Reaction to Being Possessed…Again

The voices grew louder. I couldn't keep them at bay in my recent year-and-a-half-long relationship [with Rick]. I was trying to be a good girlfriend, but he was bipolar and suicidal. Sadly, I imagine he's what it is like to date me—but times a million. My point is that this man has so many attachments, including addiction and suicidal tendencies, I'd call him a hurricane. He destroys everything in his path. In his own words: "I'm evil. I was sent here to do evil things." I tried. I really tried with him. But his attachments won't let him say one kind word to me.

I am happy to report I am sober and doing well. I haven't had any occurrences in about eight months, because I fight them off with a white light bubble that surrounds me at all times! (My daddy taught me that.) Dad was there then, with his trusty book of Jewish exorcisms. I kicked my mother, bit my father, and broke a door. But I think it's finally over—no more negative juju around anymore.

One final note: these entities want to make you look crazy and psychotic, when in fact (trust me) these entities don't attack regular people. They attach to you and attack you because you are special! You were put on this earth to do good!

Chapter 16

Spirit Box

By 2015 my relationship with God continued to expand due to meditation and extensive reading. I was convinced I had an obligation to make the tale of Brittany's possession public in an attempt to help others who found themselves in a similar situation.

But by that autumn, my creative juices were stymied with a bad case of writer's block. Floundering with my own lack of inspiration, I asked God to please "point me in the right direction." Then a few mornings later, I awoke with a pretty clear-cut plan of action.

It occurred to me to turn to Spence. I had dreamt something about Spence, but I couldn't remember what. I felt that God was trying to tell me that Spence had something to do with an ending for the book. The Irish spirit was never at a loss for words, and he might say something that would get my creative juices flowing again.

I proposed my idea to Brittany, and she seemed to think it was a solid plan. She said she'd be willing to channel Spence to see what he had to say about a possible ending. But I wanted to have a chance to prepare and to take a more scientific approach. All my reading about paranormal investigation indicated that 1) Spence's responses should be recorded, and 2) having several other people present would add validity to my conclusions about his suggestions.

I have a good friend from my theatre days named Gina Cheshire who is also very much into the paranormal. She lives in a breathtakingly restored, three-story, Victorian-era house whose haunted activity was the focus of an episode of a well-known paranormal reality TV series. Gina is originally from England and now works in the music industry in Nashville. She had known Brittany since she was a little girl and knew about her paranormal inclinations.

I thought Gina's famously haunted house would be the perfect location for Brittany to channel Spence. I approached her with the idea, and she was immediately intrigued. She had a friend, Bret Oldham, who had a spirit box and was experienced in conducting and documenting paranormal investigations. Bret has authored several books about alien abductions and has been featured on the *Ancient Aliens* TV series.

A spirit box sweeps back and forth between radio stations, so spirits can select words with which to communicate. Invented by Dr. Konstantin Raudive in the 1940s, it was further refined by Frank Sumption in 2002, and his version is sometimes called the Frank Box.

Gina had set the event for the evening before Halloween, which was totally coincidental. But *if* the veil between worlds is really thinner then, hopefully we might get even more involved information.

As the time drew closer for our EVP session, Britt seemed to be growing more apprehensive. A couple of days before we were scheduled to go to Gina's, she delivered some rather startling news.

"I don't want to channel Spence," she said. "Something doesn't feel right. He's been trying to come through a lot lately. I say no like Laurel told me I could, but he keeps trying. I don't know why, but it doesn't feel right. I'm starting to think that maybe Hans was right about Spence."

I hadn't been prepared for that one. I'd thought of Spence much as our eccentric Irish friend for sixteen years. We'd often go months or even a few years without hearing from him, but whenever Britt would channel him, it was like our humorous uncle had dropped by. If Britt was having doubts about his sincerity or that he wasn't who he claimed to be, I would totally honor her wishes.

"I'd still like to go to Gina's and see who else we might pick up," Britt volunteered.

I called Gina and filled her in, asking if maybe she'd just like to call the whole thing off. She agreed we should honor Brittany's wishes and have a spirit box session to see what other spirits might be interested in volunteering messages about the book.

Gina met us at the door of her Victorian mansion and ushered us past the wide, ornate stairway, through the parlor, into a hallway, past the dining room, and then into her kitchen fitted with modern appliances that were modified to look Victorian. It was like stepping back into 1880, with absurdly tall ceilings, ornate woodwork and moldings, period wallpaper, velvet drapes, and polished hardwood floors.

Gina's husband, Jospeh, was sitting at the kitchen table talking to three of their friends who were interested in the paranormal, including Bret, his wife, and a school teacher named Yolanda. After polite conversation as Britt and I got to know Gina's friends, we proceeded into the dining room where we'd be holding the spirit box session. We all sat around an enormous, cherry dining room table to meet people we couldn't see. Gina lit a number of candles scattered about the room and then turned the lights out. I had no idea of what to expect.

Because spirit boxes work by scanning numerous radio channels, the broadcast heard is basically pure static until that rare moment when the spirit detects a word it wants to use. You hear a few words between the static, which is quite loud and more than a bit irritating. Going around the table, the others asked personal questions to which I frankly paid little attention. Finally, it got to be my turn.

"Even though I don't have an ending yet, should I go ahead and finish the book I'm writing?" I asked my unseen friends.

There was a brief pause in the static, and then another burst of frantic static. I understood absolutely nothing, since I'm deaf in one ear.

"Well then, there's your answer then, isn't it?" Gina said in her Northern English accent.

"I have no idea what was just said," I answered. "It just sounded like static. Translation?"

Everyone, including Brittany, was tremendously excited and they were all talking at once. After they had all calmed down, I gathered that they had heard a woman's voice say something to the effect of "Finish thee the damn book."

Had that been my old friend Patience? If so, she sounded somewhat outdone with me for even asking for direction, as well as a bit snippy.

The others asked a few more questions and seemed delighted with the answers they received. Of course, I couldn't understand any of it.

I did receive two kernels of information out of the spirit box session. It appeared Patience thought the book was a good idea and that I should finish it. But the most important thing I garnered from all this was that for some unknown reason (at least to me), Brittany no longer trusted Spence and had refused to channel him again.

Spirit Ventriloquism

Almost a year after the paranormal incidents resulting in my exorcism using passages from Psalms, Britt was living at my house again. Rick was, thankfully, no longer in the picture.

One night I got up around three a.m. to go to the restroom, went inside, and closed the door. But then I heard Brittany's voice just outside: "Daddy? I have to go to the bathroom." Well, that wasn't the first time that ever happened. So I got up, ready to hold it a little longer, opened the door—and discovered there was no one there. I opened the door to Brittany's room, but she was sound asleep.

I don't always have faith in my psychic feelings, but I instinctively felt I might have just been visited by a disembodied entity of some kind mimicking Brittany's voice. This didn't feel like anything I could blame on Waya—as much as I might have wanted to.

No, the old dread I'd felt so many times before overwhelmed me, and I feared that paranormal things might be ramping up again.

A few days after this incident, Brittany told me the previous night she was sitting in her room on the computer when she heard a knock at the door. She responded with "Yeah?" and heard me say, "Can I come in?" She said, "Sure," but then I didn't enter. She said she thought maybe I was bringing clothes or something in and my hands were full. So she got up to let me in. There was no one there. Rather than go downstairs and tell me about this episode at the time, she went back to what she was doing and asked me about it the next morning. We just chalked it up to another spirit-powered incident. Waya seemed harmless, so I used him as the scapegoat. I didn't want to get her upset.

I had read demons have the ability to mimic voices and was worried an entity was planning something malicious.

More Holy Water and the Kindness of a Priest

About a month later, on February 11, at about three a.m. once again, Britt was downstairs in the kitchen talking to Facebook friends on her computer. I was upstairs sound asleep. Her desk faced the wall, and behind her were the sink and kitchen cabinets. As she plucked at the keyboard, she said she heard a "creaking" sound and looked around to see all the cabinet doors and drawers wide open. She at first thought it was our kitchen ghost, Waya, messing with her.

In a firm voice she commanded, "Stop it. You can't be here. Get out!" However, then the doors and drawers all very slowly closed as she watched. I might have taken this as a sign that Waya was acquiescing to her demands, but Brittany found the slow closing of the doors and drawers even more unsettling than hearing them all open. She was more than a little rattled and quickly turned back to her computer, telling her online friend she had to go because something weird was happening in the house. She then ran upstairs, got her shoes, and ran outside.

It was twenty-five degrees out with an inch of snow on the ground. Not even remotely dressed for inclement weather, Britt took off on her expedition while wearing pajamas, a sweater, and a pair of plastic gardening shoes. She ran about a block and a half up to the corner of the next street, stopped, and tried to figure out what to do next. She had no plan up until this point when it occurred to her that she needed holy water.

Even though it was three in the morning, she decided to walk to the nearest Catholic church—which is about half a mile from our condo. She figured no one would be there, but something told her to go.

When Britt arrived at the church, the door was locked. She knocked but there was no answer. She turned to leave and had walked about fifteen feet when a priest answered and asked if she needed help. She told him she had come to the church to get some holy water—and there was something paranormal in her house. He invited her inside where she told him the whole story of how she had been possessed fifteen years earlier. She went into as much detail as she remembered, and basically bared her soul to him.

The kindly, middle-aged priest said he usually wouldn't have been at the church that early but was there to prepare for early morning mass. He said something told him he should get there early that day. Sheepishly, Britt confessed to him that she had been Pagan for a long time after the possession—and asked if having tarot cards or other Pagan artifacts in the house could have caused this.

He strongly cautioned her to get rid of anything Pagan, including Pagan altars, whether they were currently being used or not—because they could possibly attract negative entities or demons. He said all the individual items didn't have to be thrown away (like the mementos that had belonged to her friend Tracy), but the altars, tarot cards, and Ouija boards needed to be trashed.

The Catholic priest gave her a jar of holy water and told her to go back home and bless the house. He said the most effective way was for us to do this ourselves. He gave her pretty specific instructions on what to do, and then asked if he could drive her home. But after all his wise advice, she said she still didn't want to go home. The saintly priest advised her to return and face her fears head on—that God would be with her. He assured her the holy water would protect her, and he then brought her home.

I had awoken at four a.m. and saw that Britt was nowhere to be found. The front and back doors were unlocked. I called her cellphone, afraid she'd gone off with one of her old friends who'd repetitiously made a habit of getting her into trouble. But when she answered, she sounded fine. I asked where she was.

"I'm on the road coming home. There are demons in the house. I had to get out. I was scared," she replied rather matter-of-factly. I told her to "get home right now," not really knowing what might be going on.

She said she'd been to the Catholic church to get holy water and would be back soon. About five minutes later, she did come home and had a jar of water. Britt described the paranormal events leading up to her mad dash to the Catholic church without a coat in the snow, her talk with the priest, and the instructions he gave her to bless the house and hopefully get rid of any negative entities.

I got my Bible and we went through the whole house with her sprinkling holy water and me reading the passages from Psalms I had used a year earlier. After maybe twenty minutes of this, Britt said she felt they were all gone. But just to make sure, I took the holy water and made the sign of the cross on every door and window, intoning "In the name of the Father, the Son, and the Holy Spirit" as I did so. We got upstairs, and I blessed her room and recited the Apostles' Creed. Then we said the Lord's Prayer together. By then she was sleepy, and I kissed her good night. I too went to bed, reciting the Apostles' Creed and scores of Hail Marys until I went off to sleep. I slept maybe four hours.

There were no other incidents for nearly two weeks, but then I awoke around three a.m. again one morning and pattered off to the restroom as was my usual ritual. A few seconds after I'd closed the restroom door, I heard three insistent knocks. I assumed that Brittany was on the other side of the doorway.

"Hang on, Peanut. Give me just a second," I said. Within perhaps three seconds, I found myself standing at the open door looking out into an empty hallway. I looked into Britt's room to find that she was sound asleep. I have no explanation for the knocking at the restroom door—definitely one I could not blame on the cats.

Things were relatively peaceful for the next few months. Hoping for the best, I prayed that the homemade cleansing we'd done with the priest's holy water had rid the house of negative entities—and the "knock, knock, knocking" on the bathroom door was just Waya saying hi.

Chapter 17
It Just Keeps Happening

Approximately four months later, Britt started complaining the doorknob to her bedroom had been locking itself. At various times when I'd go up to check on her, the door would be locked—something that she rarely did. The knob is an old lock meant for an exterior door. It can be unlocked with a key from one side. A few years after we'd moved into the condo, her bedroom doorknob broke off and couldn't be fixed. I had an exterior knob left over from a past remodel, so to save a few bucks I installed it on her door—although the key to it had long ago disappeared.

But not having a key didn't seem to be important, since there was never any reason to lock that door until now, when it had seemingly learned to lock itself. A few weeks earlier, I had to call my handyman to pick the lock and let me in on a day when Britt was off with friends.

Then the lock started locking itself on a regular basis. Britt learned to pick the lock, so we basically just ignored the inconvenience.

But on the evening of June 13, I went up to check on her and found things a bit wonky. Her door was locked, the light was on in my bedroom across the hall (never on unless I'm doing something up there), the window air conditioner was on (never turned on unless I intend to be in the room for a while), my ceiling fan was on (almost *never* turned on), and the light was on in the bathroom (Britt might have left that one on). I'm particular about making sure that electrical switches are turned off if the light or appliance in question is not in use. Brittany knows my habits and wouldn't have turned things on in my room.

I knocked on her door to see if she knew more than I did.

"Hang on," she replied as I heard her fidgeting with the knob. "The door's locked itself again." Then she let me in. I asked if she'd turned any of the electrical gadgets on, and she said, "No, but the doorknob to my closet has been jiggling like someone was in there trying to get out. Now this. I think maybe something is going on again."

I didn't deny there might be some kind of rekindled paranormal activity going on. I thought the best course of action was just to ignore it since it was nothing compared to what happened over a decade ago. If Waya was looking for attention, maybe he'd give up if I simply looked the other way.

I made a few jokes about the spooks not having much to do except bother us by saying, "No one is scared by this, you know. Congratulations, you can flip a few switches. Wow! What a talented Casper!" Responding with humor is almost always more effective than showing fear.

I also thought that if I displayed fear, Brittany would be more likely to also. She was infinitely more bothered by our paranormal activities than I was, and for very good reason.

After turning everything off that had switched itself on, I went back downstairs and resumed watching television. In less than half an hour, I heard banging upstairs, like furniture being moved. I rushed back upstairs to check.

I entered my room and switched on the light. One long side of my bed is always pushed up against a wall, leaving three sides exposed. The head of the bed had been shoved out away from the wall about two feet, leaving a triangular-shaped gap between bed and wall, with the foot of the bed still against the wall. I also have a director's chair in my bedroom. It's very lightweight, made of canvas and wood. It was turned over onto its side, and the rack where I keep my shoes was sitting on top of it. The shoes were all neatly removed and placed in a line on a coffee table I keep next to my bed. My belts had been neatly rolled up next to each other, with various bottles of nose spray and eye drops placed inside the coiled belts. A pair of house shoes, which I'd yet to even wear, was dangling from the shoe rack hanging by the plastic string that still held the shoes together. Anchored between the coffee table and the director's chair was a painting Brittany had done years ago for me. It had been hanging above my dresser about six feet from where it currently sat. The display in its entirety was actually very well executed and almost artistically done. But at the time, I didn't appreciate the artistry.

I called for Brittany to come see this latest creation and could see that she was noticeably upset and more than a little scared.

For her sake, I should have kept my cool, but these spirit prank-sters were starting to get on my nerves. Knowing I shouldn't, I got mad and started yelling. I told it that I wasn't scared of it and if it wanted a fight it had come to the right place. Britt said that I shouldn't let it get to me, because that was "just what it wanted."

I agreed and softened my approach. I recited the Apostles' Creed and said, "In the name of the Father, the Son, and the Holy Spirit, I command you to leave." Britt went back to her room and I went back downstairs. Everything seemed to get back to normal, and within a half an hour, she yelled down that she was going to bed.

Maybe another hour later, I went up to bed and was greeted by another elaborate display. I keep a Bible and a stack of magazines on the bathroom cabinet by the sink. They had all been relocated to the floor and painstakingly stacked with the toiletry items on the cabinet neatly surrounding the books in a circle on the floor. There were pill bottles, Brittany's various makeup items, and five or six CDs that had originally been stacked next to the CD player in the corner of the cabinet.

It looked like the entity was still trying to get my attention. I retrieved my Bible from the stack the entity had so artfully ar-ranged and turned to the book of Psalms. I have all the passages from our previous cleansing marked, so I began reading them out loud. I walked from the bathroom, through the hall, and into my bedroom reading five of these poetic verses.

I also included my own little prayer that I came up with several years earlier at times when I felt negative entities were trying to in-fluence Brittany again or establish themselves in my home. It goes something like this:

"Almighty God, I hereby cast out, banish, and expel all negative or evil entities or attachments from my universe, my dimension, or my reality. That includes the universe, dimension, and reality of my daughter Brittany as our universes overlap.

"I cast you out; I banish you; I expel you; and I send you back to God Almighty, where I'm sure you will be shown kindness, warmth, and love—but that is up to God. In the name of the Father, the Son, and the Holy Spirit, I cast you out."

I went to bed and continued to recite the Apostles' Creed laced with the odd Hail Mary in my head until I fell asleep.

Cats and Big Bads Don't Mix

About four weeks passed without further incident—with the exception of one slight change in the household. Starting the very next day, one of my cats refused to go upstairs. I mention this episode because this particular cat, Little Baast, has stayed upstairs 80 percent of the time since he came to me ten years ago as a tiny kitten. My five cats have different areas of the house they particularly prefer. Baby (Brittany's cat and the oldest at twenty years now) mostly wiles away her time in Brittany's room; Samhain generally can be found in the kitchen, sleeping in my chair or chasing her tail; Dinky (an obese Russian Blue) likes to stay downstairs near the major food source; and Mr. Bean (a Bobcat-sized alpha male) generally goes wherever he likes.

But Little Baast has always spent the great majority of his time upstairs, so much so that I started putting his own food dish up there. He has slept with me near the head of the bed every night for years. However, at the ripe old age of ten, he suddenly decided to stay downstairs during the day and sleep in the kitchen at night instead of with me.

He would not go upstairs after the "Night of the Shoe and Book Display."

However, none of the other cats seemed much affected. In fact, all four of them would go back and forth from the upstairs to the downstairs areas as need be with impunity—totally unaffected by the teleportation going on that night upstairs. Baby still went upstairs to visit Brittany, and all the other cats still kept their upstairs passports valid.

The only explanation I can come up with as to why Little Baast suddenly didn't want to go upstairs is that he was in my bedroom and witnessed the entity repositioning my footwear and reading material. He very possibly saw shoes, the shoe rack, and books flying through the air. Seeing the bed he had slept in for a decade dance across the floor on its own may have been the last straw. The other cats were all downstairs during this display of teleportation and were totally unperturbed by it.

Originally named Didley, of all my cats, Little Baast is the biggest scaredy-cat. When he was young, he used to be afraid of the ten feral cats I would feed outside. Once, he got out and was gone from home for a month. I'd see him in the condo courtyard, but he couldn't work up the courage to cross the feral picket line to get back inside, no matter how much I called. Then one day he just appeared from out of nowhere in my bedroom. I still have no idea how he got in. Perhaps he zipped behind me undetected one day as I stood on the porch calling him, or maybe ... I half-jokingly concluded he was magic and renamed him "Little Baast" after the Egyptian demigod.

I believe that my reading of the Psalms, the Apostles' Creed, and all the Hail Marys got rid of my uninvited guests, but Little Baast wasn't predisposed to take any chances. I'd watch him look out the front window, possibly considering whether it might be safer to brave the feral cats or take a chance upstairs—always wondering if the shoes might start dancing again.

I Hear You Knockin'

I went to bed around midnight after first opening the door to Brittany's room, looking in on her, and seeing she was sound asleep. After I crossed over into my bedroom, I noticed that a chair had been moved out from the wall about three feet. I didn't remember moving it and was sure that if I had, I would have put it back in its usual place. I joked to the spirits or the universe in general, "That's not where that goes. If you're going to rearrange the décor, learn to put things back."

Lately I had been feeling low on energy without any desire to get much of anything done. The low energy didn't affect my work, but anything that took much physical exertion was getting put off till later. I was tired and eager to go to bed.

However after talking to Brittany the next morning, I learned there were a lot of things happening that night I didn't know about.

At the time, Britt mostly stayed upstairs in her room where she had her computer, TV, and movies. My office is downstairs, so I'm either working on the computer or watching TV. We usually checked on each other every few hours, and life went on.

But that morning, she hesitatingly told me that at one point the night before, she thought she'd heard me come to her door and knock. She told me to come in—and she heard me say, "I can't. It's locked." Since her door had been locking itself that summer, this seemed like a normal reply, so she'd gotten up to unlock it and let me in. The door was *not* locked—and I was not there. She also said she heard me in my bedroom moving things and talking to the cats. That also did not happen. All the cats and I were downstairs at the time.

The most disturbing part was that Britt was hearing a voice again imitating my voice, and it looked like things were firing up once again.

By this time, I had been thinking that since we had banished negative entities with holy water and blessed the house with the reading of Psalms and the Apostles' Creed, maybe it was time to rethink my battle plans.

Chapter 18
The Reboot

After all these recent events, maybe I had missed something concerning the case.

Laurel had told us years ago that the house wasn't haunted. According to her, Brittany was acting as a lightning rod drawing all these spirits in, be they human or demonic. Her theory was that even if we moved, the spirits/demons would happily accompany us—because they were attracted to Brittany no matter where we might go.

But what if Laurel was wrong? She had selflessly come to our aid and done an exorcism/cleansing when officials of several churches had turned their backs on us—and for that, I will always be eternally grateful. For the most part, Laurel's exorcism had worked; we all owed her a great deal. However, Brittany had been plagued by spirits (and possibly demons) off and on for sixteen years. Even after Britt had gotten married and moved out, my condo still seemed to be haunted by something. The spiritual activity was never as intense when Britt wasn't staying here, but paranormal events continued to occur. Could the condo itself be haunted?

There were things going bump in the night here, at least occasionally, regardless of whether Brittany was on the scene.

I was basing all my conclusions about our haunting on what one psychic had told me many years ago. I wasn't applying the rules of good journalism to my own case. My investigation hadn't gone far enough and was incomplete. Some piece was missing from the puzzle.

All those years ago there were very few paranormal investigating groups in the area offering help to victims of hauntings or possessions, but it's a new day, and attitudes toward the paranormal have drastically changed.

The internet has opened up a whole new universe of information. Compared to the way we did research in the seventies, it almost seemed like magic. I started looking for paranormal investigators in our area on the internet. There were eight or ten to choose from, but after checking all their websites, the most promising seemed to be s4p Paranormal, a paranormal investigation team headed up by a psychic named Renee Anderson.

The group is an all-female investigative team, and I thought Brittany might respond better to an all-female group. She usually seemed to make a better emotional connection with women.

I sent an email to a team member named Melody Cole and gave a rather lengthy description of what had been going on with us over the previous sixteen years. The very next day I got an answer from a member of the team named Lisa Jordan who turned out to be the one in charge of setting up investigations. Lisa said they were intrigued and they'd like to come out and talk to Brittany and me. We set a date in August 2016.

Lisa and Renee arrived about one p.m., and we all sat down at the kitchen table to discuss the case. Renee especially didn't want to hear too much background information concerning the events of sixteen years ago. Being the group's psychic, she wanted to be able to walk through the house and try to pick up her own readings of what might be going on. She didn't want to be prejudiced by too much verbal information and was more interested in present paranormal activity than what had happened in the past.

After she'd listened to the very basics of our present paranormal shenanigans, Renee announced she was going to do a walk-through by herself, while Brittany and I talked to Lisa. She described what the group would be doing, including the electronic tests they'd be running, and had us sign a consent form.

Melody arrived and joined the group at the kitchen table while Renee was upstairs. She knew a bit more about the background of the case since I'd done most of my initial email correspondence with her and had talked with her on the phone a couple of times.

After maybe twenty minutes, Renee returned and sat back down with us.

"You definitely have some activity here," she announced. "There are at least two spirits who stay here all the time. One of them can't leave, and the other one just doesn't want to."

She went on to explain that there was a tall man with a "big hat and a long coat" who stays at the top of the stairs. The physical description of him being "tall" made me think of Waya, the Native American spirit—and maybe the "big hat" was the headdress I'd seen. Britt had also been saying for years that there was a very tall man in "some kind of costume" she'd see around the house, especially in the kitchen. She said she was pretty sure he didn't like her.

Renee said the man at the top of the stairs likes it up there because he can look down and see everything else that's going on. That reminded me of an incident that happened not long after Tracy had died. Brittany was coming down the stairs one evening and fell forward, losing her balance and stumbling down four steps before she caught herself. I heard her falling and got there about the time she hit the last step. She said at the time she felt like she'd "been pushed." That kind of subjective experience is really difficult to validate—so not much was made of it. Neither Britt nor I are exactly what you'd call graceful, so I just let it go.

But Renee agreed that the spirit may very well have shoved Brittany, and said it definitely was not a benevolent spirit. I asked if she knew his name.

"I didn't ask," she said. "When I get the feeling that they're negative spirits, I don't ask questions. I only speak to wicked spirits through my own spirit guides. It's safer for me that way. They told me what he was up to. I just know the evil ones are not supposed to be here. This guy is a very bad dude. He's causing unrest upstairs and down."

Renee also said she went into the bathroom and encountered a little girl about sixteen years old.

"She doesn't know why she's here," Renee revealed. "She said she had two sisters and lived on a farm nearby. I think her father was a sharecropper. They struggled financially, and she argued with her mother frequently because she didn't want to grow up and settle for what her mother had. Of course, her mother couldn't understand that. She died in a farming accident—maybe something to do with a hay wagon. The girl got stuck here about five years ago for some reason. Before that she could move around the area, but she's stuck here now and can't leave."

Britt had moved back in with me about seven years earlier. Maybe her psychic lightning rod attracted the girl and she couldn't get away. Renee also said the little girl was afraid of the bad dude at the top of the stairs.

It's also worth mentioning that since Brittany moved back in, she's complained that she sees a little girl in the bathroom that "looks a lot like me as a teenager—but she has on a long dress and she's covered in blood." The girl Renee described had on a long dress and had been killed in a farming accident—hence, the blood. I'm also theorizing that if the little girl resembled Brittany, that might explain why Britt's psychic lightning rod pulled her in.

Renee told Britt that the girl said to tell her she was sorry if she had scared her.

Also, somewhat to my surprise, Renee said she detected the spirit of my grandfather who was there to protect us against any negative entities. From her description of his personality, I ascertained that this would have been my father's father. She said I had been very close to him, but that could have applied to either of my grandfathers. But when she said he was an assertive, gregarious soul used to getting his own way and had adored me when I was little, I knew which one she meant. *That* granddad had died when I was only five, but I distinctly remember him fetching me once a week in his green '54 Ford pickup truck to take me to the drug store to get ice cream and a comic book. He had died of a stroke at sixty-five while working on his farm. I was relieved to know he was watching over us, but not really surprised.

I had often thought I could feel his presence. In fact, it wasn't unusual for me to ask for advice from him when I'd find myself in yet another unenviable situation.

However, I was quite surprised when Renee said she felt that Brittany and I both had attachments as a result of all the spiritual activity of the last decade and a half. I frankly wasn't that shocked to learn that Brittany still had a few hitchhikers (that's what this was all about in the first place), but I was flabbergasted to hear that uninvited guests had landed on *me*.

The ladies from s4p Paranormal set up an appointment to come and run their various electronic paranormal tests for a Saturday night in September. They said we'd have to spend the night somewhere else and find a place to keep the cats. I frankly wasn't too excited about trying to find somewhere to lodge five cats.

The Final Cleansing

Lisa emailed me several times before the group was set to come back in September to check if there had been any further activity since their first visit. Oddly enough, there *hadn't* been any further paranormal episodes. Things had been so unusually quiet; I felt like I was living somewhere else. The quiet we'd been experiencing for several weeks truly surprised me, because they didn't really *do* anything on their first visit except talk to us.

I mentioned the relative serenity we were experiencing to Lisa, and she said that would often happened after the group's first visit to a home experiencing spirit activity.

"Sometimes I believe that the spirits think that if they just lay low for a while, maybe we won't come back," Lisa explained. "Frequently people tell us things have calmed down; but trust me, it won't last."

Then about a week before the s4p group was scheduled to come back and take their various electronic readings and pictures, Lisa sent me an email saying they had met as a group to talk about our case. They had decided that there wasn't any reason to set up all that electronic paranormal equipment to prove there was spiritual activity going on at our condo. Renee had walked through the house and detected two spirits and even talked with one of them. Since Britt and I had witnessed active paranormal activity bouncing off the walls here for years, *we* sure didn't need any physical proof.

As a result, they wouldn't need to stay here an entire night with all their equipment churning away picking up evidence. Lisa said they would like to come and have Renee remove the attachments from Britt and me and then cleanse the home. The whole process would only take about four hours. This made perfect sense to me. Why waste time and equipment to prove something we all already agreed was happening?

This time only Renee and Lisa came to the condo. While Renee went upstairs to explain to our teenaged ghost what was about to happen and that she had no reason to be afraid, Lisa took Britt and me into the kitchen for the removal of my attachment.

She lit some sage and walked around me several times, fanning the smoke on me with two feathers while repeating a prayer of cleansing. After she'd finished, she asked if I felt different, and I replied that I felt "lighter." I would also notice marked behavioral changes within a day or two.

As Lisa was finishing the cleansing ritual with me, Renee returned from her talk upstairs with the teenaged spirit.

Renee followed almost exactly the same ritual to remove Brittany's attachment that Lisa had with me. She walked around her with the sage and used the feathers to encourage it to encompass her. The removal of Britt's attachment took longer than my own because Britt's unwanted guest was more solidly attached. Also Renee told me later (because she didn't want to upset Brittany), one of Britt's attachments was what she called a "low level demon"—not higher level big bads like she'd had at fifteen, but still an unwanted trouble maker.

But it was still a relatively short ritual and nothing even remotely as traumatic as the exorcism we'd gone through with Laurel sixteen years earlier. When Renee was satisfied that the attachment was no longer connected to Brittany, she told us she needed to "rebalance Brittany's chakras" and "realign her energy centers," as the attachment(s) had caused an imbalance.

Renee, who is a Reiki Master, had Brittany lie on the floor. She then placed different healing stones near Britt's seven chakras. The different chakras are represented by seven different colors, so the colors of the stones coordinated with the colors of the chakras. As she balanced each chakra, she touched the appropriate stone to the proper region of Britt's body and made a few comments about Britt's health concerning that chakra. The one I particularly remember was when she reached the forehead, usually called the "third eye."

"You have an unusual sensitivity to sensing or seeing spirits," observed Renee.

After balancing Britt's chakras, Renee and Lisa went through the entire condo with the sage, smudging it from top to bottom, paying special attention to windows and doors. I could hear them reciting prayers of cleansing.

The condo had been cleansed, and we had been cleansed of our attachments. Renee said our two resident ghosts were also gone. She helped the teenaged spirit cross over and banished the guy at the top of the stairs, whom I, at the time, assumed was the entity I called Waya.

Waya and I had coexisted for at least ten years, and frankly had gotten along amicably. But he didn't seem to like Brittany for some reason—and more importantly, he scared her. Renee was insistent that disembodied spirits are not supposed to share the same space with us—so I figured Waya was also evicted.

Renee then asked if there was anything else they could do to help, so I asked if there would be any way she could help my grandfather cross over and go to the light.

"It really makes me sad that he hasn't crossed over," I said. "He's been dead for sixty-two years. My grandmother died in '74, and he even has several children who have passed on by now." I asked her why he'd lingered so long.

"Time isn't the same to spirits as it is to us," she said. "That may seem like a long time to you, but not nearly so long to them. He's been watching over you and others in your family as well—and there may have been other issues. I don't know. We can cross him over if you want, but we'll have to go outside. Now that the house is cleansed, he can't come back in unless you invite him, and then you're just opening a portal for other entities to get in. I definitely wouldn't advise that."

We went out back into the little courtyard. I held Renee's hands while she said a few prayers I didn't recognize. I had been mesmerized by the whole ceremony, but when I heard her say amen, I snapped out of it, repeated amen, and crossed myself like a good Episcopalian. Renee smiled and proclaimed that Granddaddy had gone on to the other side.

I felt better about his transformation but mentioned I would miss him.

"Oh, he can come back now that he's crossed," she said, "and it won't open up a door for something bad." She said it was her experience that spirits who have crossed over usually take a few days to a few weeks to adjust to their new situation.

"Don't expect him back for a while," she said. "Let him get used to things and catch up with loved ones."

As the four of us went back into the condo, I told Renee and Lisa that I wanted to make a small donation to s4p Paranormal. But before I could even get half of my proposal out, Renee stopped me.

"Thanks, but we don't want your money," she said. "We don't do this for the money."

"But it says on your website that you accept donations," I sputtered. "So I want to make a donation."

"Sorry, we won't take it," Renee said with a smile.

And they wouldn't, no matter how hard I tried to give it to them. To me, this spoke volumes about their sincerity and purpose. They do what they do because they want to help people.

As they were getting ready to go, I asked Renee who the spirits were and how they had attached themselves to us.

"My guides take care of that. I don't talk to the bad guys," she replied. "The guides just tell me they're there. They communicate with negative spirits, so I don't have to. That way I can stay focused on the light."

Good enough for me. I was just glad they'd been evicted. Renee then gave Britt and me each a black stone, slightly bigger than a quarter, called tourmaline. She said these stones would continue to protect us against negative entities trying to get back in. I keep mine in a small plastic box on my bed stand. Brittany keeps hers in her pocket. I learned from my class in Wicca that black is considered the protective color, and that is actually the reason priests have worn black since the early days of Christianity. I guess you can't argue with something that has worked for millennia.

Standing in our front door, Renee told us to let them know how things felt later and to feel free to call them if there were ever anymore paranormal disturbances. Profusely thanking Renee and Lisa, we said our farewells and watched the ladies begin their drive home.

The atmosphere in the condo was almost immediately lighter after the ladies from s4p Paranormal had done their thing. If you've ever watched a paranormal TV show about a house cleansing, you'll probably respond with "That's what they all say." But Brittany and I truly noticed an airy and tranquil feel in the condo as soon as they'd driven off.

The days that followed would be just as peaceful.

Maybe My Attachment Had OCD

After about three weeks had passed, I received an email from Renee checking up on us. I replied that there had been no further paranormal activities; the overall atmosphere felt infinitely lighter; the cats were happily going to any part of the house they wanted; and I had noticed a personal difference.

"I think my attachment had obsessive-compulsive disorder," I wrote back, only half joking.

I described how that during the last couple of years I had developed little obsessive-compulsive tics I had never had before. For example, I had gotten into the habit of tapping the on button eight times to switch certain electronic things on—rather than the once that is necessary. I don't know where this came from. I had never felt the compulsion to do anything like that before in my over sixty years. I simply chalked it up to being part of getting old.

But within a day of the house cleansing and the attachment removals, my obsessive-compulsive tics were absolutely gone. I no longer felt the compulsion to hit the on button eight times, and there were a couple of other tics that also just vanished—almost like, well, magic.

I also told Renee I thought I knew generally when my attachment had hopped on board. About eight years earlier, I had been involved with a movie project for which I had written the screenplay. It had *almost* taken flight but fell apart due to 2008's Great Recession.

With my income drastically reduced, I went into a pretty serious depression for over a year. I've read that spirit attachments feed off depression and negative thoughts, so I was ripe for the taking. The depression finally ended when Brittany moved back in with me after her divorce. Helping her get back on track with her life, and also dealing with the escalating paranormal activity precipitated by her move back in, caused me to stop wallowing in self-pity.

Sensitives Must Always Keep Their Guards Up

Almost a year after s4p's cleansing, Britt started drinking again. Demons or simply ill-intentioned human spirits prey on the weak. Since I'm not as psychic as Britt, they can knock on my door all day long and I won't respond because I don't often perceive them. But very psychically sensitive souls always need to keep their barriers up, guarding against demonic or evil attachments.

I knew Britt was drinking, but she was thirty-two years old and I wouldn't stop her if that's what she wanted to do. However, one morning she came to me and showed me several large bruises on her arms and legs. She said she had no idea how they had gotten there. She woke up the morning before, and there they were. Naturally, I feared the paranormal worst. I told her to take photos of the marks and send them to Renee.

I also talked to her about her drinking problem. I asked if perhaps she'd obtained the bruises while inebriated. But she staunchly denied that. Taking a different route, I reminded her that demons and other spirits often jump individuals who are in a weakened state like intoxication. She agreed and swore to give up her drinking.

Those bruises scared her to the point that I think she may be serious about keeping her guard up this time. Renee has also agreed to work with Brittany to help her develop her psychic abilities. This is what I had hoped for when Laurel offered to help her learn to use them many years ago, but maybe this time Renee can show her how to protect herself from the ill-intentioned entities that seem to be attracted to her.

Brittany is currently working as a caregiver for the elderly—a job she trained for years ago, when she was married. She seems to enjoy this and is more fulfilled by it than any position I've known her to have. Maybe this will be the start of a new career.

She has also started going to church on occasion, recently expressing the need for some kind of spiritual base. Over the years, she's become more comfortable with the informal and laid-back services of the Unity Church (with their emphasis on positive thinking), so she's been going there off and on. We've also been participating in a Spiritual Development Institute congregation, a metaphysical group of believers, with Renee and Lisa. The SDI emphasizes the belief in a god or universal creator of some kind and your personal contact with the universe, regardless of exactly what your concept of that original creative force might be.

Someday Britt may want to develop her psychic gifts so that she can help others, but she hasn't reached that pinnacle yet. She has expressed serious apprehensions about channeling—afraid that the effort might open up portals for our old pal/possible enemy Spence to make an inglorious return. Perhaps one day she'll feel confident enough to develop her abilities so that she can protect herself while still helping others—and perhaps not. After what she's gone through for nearly two decades, I can understand her not wanting to take the chance. I totally support her in whatever final decision she makes.

For Whom the Fear Tolls

Although our paranormal disturbances bothered Brittany infinitely more than they did me, I have to admit that I have had my own fear factor to deal with. The haunting has taken an emotional toll on me as well. The worst of it was, of course, during the initial possession eighteen years ago—and off and on for a year thereafter. Although I kept my cool at the times of my various discussions with demons as channeled through Brittany, these were the most terrifying incidents of my life.

William Peter Blatty has said that he wrote *The Exorcist* not with the intention of scaring anyone, but to express a "testimony of faith." By illustrating the epitome of evil as represented by the demon in his book and subsequent film, Blatty's primary purpose was to highlight the faith of the priests who vanquished it—and thus, to act as examples for others.

My own real-life experience paralleled this in some rather profound ways. At a time when my faith was at a seriously low ebb, I had to muster all the spiritual stamina I could to assure that my daughter would not be taken. I suppose I literally "talked to the devil." By doing so, my faith in God would eventually be renewed—although the renewal process spanned at least another decade.

But there was fear. Even though I might have projected an outward image of composure, bravura, and even humor to Brittany when we'd be in the midst of paranormal activity—inwardly I could hear my proverbial teeth chattering. Even after nearly three years of peace and quiet, every time I wake up during the night I instinctively recite the Apostles' Creed over and over again until I drift back off to sleep.

Chapter 19

Possible Explanation

Laurel told us back in 2001 that the house was not haunted—Brittany was. She was attracting spirits, both good and bad, like moths to a flame. Just to double check on the haunted house theory, I researched the history of the property the condo is built on and found there was never anything else here. The land had been part of a horse farm.

But about a month after Renee's cleansing, I was approached with another possible solution to the spiritual turmoil that had occurred here.

I had become friends with a Liberal Catholic bishop (which is not affiliated with the Roman Catholic Church, and does allow women to be ordained), and although I rarely bring up the story about Brittany's possession with *anyone*, I somehow felt that I could ask Carol about it. After hearing a condensed version of the story you've just read, Bishop Carol said that she had no doubt that paranormal activities do take place, including demonic possessions. She then confessed, "I don't tell just everyone this, but I'm psychic." She asked me to tell her about the condo we live in, saying she was "getting a bad feeling about the land." I replied with a summary of the dead end I'd come up against trying to research the property. "Looks like it was nothing but farmland and horses."

However, the bishop said she was getting "a very strong and compelling feeling that all this wasn't caused by your daughter. It's the land. Something's wrong with the land." She said that the problem goes back centuries to the Native Americans.

"There was a curse, or maybe something spiritually protective put on it," she explained. "It's hallowed ground. People may be buried there. I get the feeling that no one should ever live there."

That would explain quite a bit. The first thing coming to mind, of course, is my vanquished Native American spirit Waya. Maybe Waya was protecting something here sacred to his people. Tracy also told us she had seen ghosts in her condo on numerous occasions. When I first moved in twenty-four years ago, Dianne, the lady living next door then, mentioned that she thought her condo was haunted. She'd seen spirits and swore that small objects often turned up in places other than where she put them. Brittany became friends with her daughter, Marlo, who also described seeing "misty figures or spirits" upstairs on the landing.

Britt says that when she'd stay at her mom's house when she was young, she'd occasionally see spirits, but nothing to the extent that she did here in the condo. *And*, when she was married and living with Kevin, she still occasionally saw apparitions—but that nothing ever felt as threatening to her as it did here.

If the bishop is right and my condo sits on a sacred (or cursed) Native American site, then we may have been dealing with elemental spirits who protect and manipulate the forces of nature.

They figure prominently in nature-based Pagan religions in their many forms, including the European Celts, African, and Norse religions, and Native American shamanism.

They are "chaotic spirits," in that they do not differentiate between our concept of good and evil.

Therefore, if the old condo here is sitting on top of sacred Native American grounds guarded by one or more elementals, you can't help but wonder if our paranormal shenanigans over the years (and even the possession itself) could be attributed to one or more elementals.

Another similarity that comes to mind is the nineteenth-century haunting of the Bell Witch. Many who've researched that case have concluded that the spirit, Kate, was an elemental summoned to guard the land by Native Americans. Kate displayed both kind and cruel characteristics. She tortured the daughter, Betsy Bell, and is even said to have murdered the patriarch of the Bell family, John. Nevertheless, the spirit often showed kindness, especially to the mother, Lucy. Many who claim to have heard Kate actually speak attested to her wry sense of humor.

If the entity we came to know as Spence was actually our demon (as Renee and the voodoo shaman Hans believe), he displayed striking similarities to the Bell Witch in many ways. If Spence was a chaotic elemental spirit, it would explain his cruel possession of Brittany—as juxtaposed to his outwardly good-natured sense of humor and friendly personality. Maybe Spence had us fooled for nearly two decades into thinking he was some kind of guardian angel for Brittany. But if Spence was the demonic or elemental entity that possessed Britt when she was fifteen, his evil side far overshadowed his witty repartee.

I don't believe Spence would have ever entered our lives if our use of my old Ouija board hadn't opened a portal to his dimension. But evil entities can be prevented from using the board as a portal, and the Ouija board can be an effective way to communicate with positive human entities no longer in physical form. However, the sessions must be properly protected beforehand and properly closed at the end.

And perhaps I was warned of all this. In one Ouija board session twenty years before Brittany ever touched one, an entity told me to guard "the wee one." Those twenty years might have seemed a very long time to me, but to some demonic entity (possibly Spence?) it was but a cosmic breath in quantum time. Did this demonic entity lay in wait until just the right moment to pounce on Brittany when she started playing with the Ouija board? I sincerely wish I knew.

It is difficult to believe that anyone as affable and seemingly good-natured as Spence could have been a demon, but they say that psychopaths often display a persona of affable humor and good will—just before they stab you in the back.

Conclusion

The night of the original possession was the most traumatic night of our lives. I still have nightmares about it. It was something that I wouldn't wish on my worst enemy. One hellish night scarred the members of our family in ways that couldn't possibly be fully understood by anyone other than someone who had gone through an actual possession themselves. But in particular, it decimated the life of Brittany.

She had never liked school and made average to slightly below-average grades before the possession. But afterward, academics were a drudgingly overwhelming uphill climb. She couldn't get her mind off what had happened to her long enough to give mathematics or history much consideration. Depression was her constant companion, no matter whom she was with or where she went. Britt developed a chip on her shoulder and was prone to getting into frequent fights at school. Her grades plummeted.

Brittany had also never had any kind of emotional problem before the possession. She was the life of the party in most situations and was gifted with an incredible personality and sense of humor.

But after the possession, her depression took her to the depths of hell and left her once perky self-confidence in shambles. She has been under the care of four different psychiatrists since the age of fifteen and in and out of psychiatric hospitals (always for brief stays) on five or six occasions. As a teenager, she became a cutter as a way of using physical pain to overpower her emotional pain. Even after her marriage, she needed so much attention that she repeatedly cheated on her husband, causing that chance at happiness to dissolve after five years. How many of Britt's emotional problems were caused by the possession, and how many would have surfaced anyway? Your guess is as good as mine.

However, we finally found a top-notch psychiatrist who diagnosed her emotional problems (the depression, the bipolar tendencies) as the result of the possession. Dr. Beth Baxter has adjusted Britt's medication accordingly, and she's doing better now than she has in years.

Between her finally getting a psychiatrist who admits that the possession really happened and Renee's cleansing of the condo, things are finally starting to look promising for the first time in many years.

But what really was it? What caused the possession? I wish I had definitive answers, but I can only guess. I choose to call the example that plagued our family a demon because it possessed Brittany's body, and because that has been the phrase used to describe evil, disembodied entities possessing humans since before the time of Jesus Christ. Was it a fallen angel? Possibly. I do believe such beings exist, but I do not know without a shadow of doubt if that is what took over her body. I only know for sure that something did.

Scientists are learning more and more every day about the building blocks of the universe. Newtonian physics is being rapidly superseded by quantum physics. Newton's simple gravity-controlled apple is now thought to be a complicated combination of spinning subatomic protons and electrons. Indeed, the physical apple may very well not visually exist unless it is *observed*. Sounds crazy, but the enormous, underground Hadron Collider in Europe is proving that visual interaction with material objects is required for them to exist in a physical format. Scientists also believe this is the beginning of proof that the physical world is not what we think it is, and that other dimensions do indeed exist and can be proven mathematically. Shakespeare said in *Hamlet* that "there are more things in heaven and earth, Horatio, than are dreamt of in your philosophy." Maybe the Bard was onto something from both a spiritual standpoint and a scientific one.

I personally believe that science will soon hold answers to religious and metaphysical questions—things that have been explained for thousands of years as arguable mysticism may one day be proven scientifically. One day not so far in the future, magic may prove to be a set of scientific principles we simply don't, at this time, understand.

How does that relate to the demonic entities that possess human beings from time to time? I believe that demons (be they fallen angels, elemental nature spirits, or interdimensional travelers) will someday be proven to be scientifically measurable entities, enabling us to learn to banish them in a more effective and permanent way.

Renee believes that real demonic possessions are quite rare. However, that doesn't reflect my personal experiences with evil demonic entities, and that's all I have to go on. Whatever they are, they are evil, they are disruptive, and they are *not* supposed to be here.

Brittany was ultimately scarred by the possession that radically changed the course of her life back in 2001. Her teen years can't be given back to her, and I'll always feel that all this was essentially my fault. I am the one, after all, who introduced her to the Ouija board.

My only defense is that my own introduction to the Ouija board did not include proper protection techniques from evil entities beforehand and safe closure afterward. I saw the Ouija board as a positive thing, just as my early mentor, Eileen, did. I don't think it ever occurred to Eileen or her mother, Pearl, that such protection was even necessary. Pearl had used the board as a tool to communicate with the spirit of Patience Worth; Patience used it as a tool to write her novels and poems. There were no demons, no evil spirits.

Effects on My Own Spiritual Journey

If only one soul who is being plagued by a demonic entity reads this and is helped in some way by it, then it was worth the time and effort it took me to write this book. If another family can use the information I gathered to lessen their pain in some way, then it was worth it.

At the time of Brittany's possession, I had strayed from any real relationship with God. It took a journey through pure hell—watching a demon steal the joy from my daughter's life and almost destroy her sanity—to rediscover my faith. Few people can claim to have talked to a demon, but I am a member of that exclusive and unenviable club. I'll never forget that day in the car with Brittany on a two-lane road with water on both sides and nowhere to pull over. Her eyes turned black as she began channeling a demon. I was so scared I put my vocal cords on automatic pilot and let God do the talking. Instinctively, I called upon the only power I knew who could save us. God, the source of all life in the universe, told me the right things to say. The demon left my daughter that night because I guaranteed that if it would return to God, it would find love, reconciliation, final forgiveness, and ultimate salvation—rather than the eternal damnation it expected. The forgiveness I described to the demon resonated just as soundly with me.

Sadly I had to see the evil a demon could do and the emotional carnage it could cause before I could truly reach out to the creative source of the universe.

Our ordeal with demonic entities has been horrifying at times and enraging at times, but ultimately enlightening. It took a terrifying experience with a demon and the near loss of my daughter's soul to help me find God, but I pray that you're not as stubborn or as hardheaded as I was. God bless and keep you in your journey through life.

To Write the Author

If you wish to contact the author or would like more information about this book, please write to the author in care of Llewellyn Worldwide, and we will forward your request. Both the author and publisher appreciate hearing from you and learning of your enjoyment of this book and how it has helped you. Llewellyn Worldwide cannot guarantee that every letter written to the author can be answered, but all will be forwarded. Please write to:

William Dorian
% Llewellyn Worldwide
2143 Wooddale Drive
Woodbury, MN 55125.2989

Please enclose a self-addressed stamped envelope for reply, or $1.00 to cover costs. If outside the U.S.A., enclose an international postal reply coupon.

GET MORE AT LLEWELLYN.COM

Visit us online to browse hundreds of our books and decks, plus sign up to receive our e-newsletters and exclusive online offers.

- • Free tarot readings • Spell-a-Day • Moon phases
- • Recipes, spells, and tips • Blogs • Encyclopedia
- • Author interviews, articles, and upcoming events

GET SOCIAL WITH LLEWELLYN

Find us on  🐦 @LlewellynBooks

www.Facebook.com/LlewellynBooks

GET BOOKS AT LLEWELLYN

LLEWELLYN ORDERING INFORMATION

Order online: Visit our website at www.llewellyn.com to select your books and place an order on our secure server.

Order by phone:
- • Call toll free within the US at 1-877-NEW-WRLD (1-877-639-9753)
- • We accept VISA, MasterCard, American Express, and Discover.

Order by mail:
Send the full price of your order (MN residents add 6.875% sales tax) in US funds plus postage and handling to: Llewellyn Worldwide, 2143 Wooddale Drive, Woodbury, MN 55125-2989

POSTAGE AND HANDLING

STANDARD (US):(Please allow 12 business days)
$30.00 and under, add $6.00.
$30.01 and over, FREE SHIPPING.

CANADA:
We cannot ship to Canada, please shopyour local bookstore or Amazon Canada.

INTERNATIONAL:
Customers pay the actual shipping cost to the final destination, which includes tracking information.

Visit us online for more shipping options.
Prices subject to change.

FREE CATALOG!

To order, call
1-877-
NEW-WRLD
ext. 8236
or visit our
website

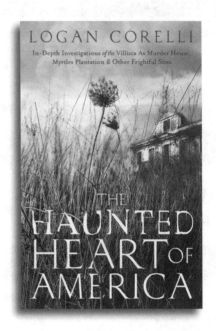

LOGAN CORELLI

In-Depth Investigations *of the* Villisca Ax Murder House,
Myrtles Plantation & Other Frightful Sites

THE
HAUNTED
HEART OF
AMERICA

The Haunted Heart of America

In-Depth Investigations of the Villisca Ax Murder House, Myrtles Plantation & Other Frightful Sites

LOGAN CORELLI

In the heartland, tales of grisly deaths and unsolved murders abound—and the spirits of the dead are often left behind. Join Logan Corelli and his teams as they explore some of the creepiest haunted locations in America, where spirits and entities terrify even the most experienced investigators.

The Haunted Heart of America provides tantalizing evidence of realms of existence beyond our own. Featuring firsthand investigations of famous paranormal hotspots like Waverly Hills, Myrtles Plantation, and the St. James Hotel—as well as many lesser-known though equally fascinating locations—this riveting book shares spine-chilling stories, hair-raising experiences, and fascinating physical evidence.

978-0-7387-5591-5, 240 pp., 5¼ x 8   **$16.99**

NOMAR SLEVIK

OTHERWORLDLY
ENCOUNTERS

EVIDENCE
OF
UFO SIGHTINGS
AND
ABDUCTIONS

Otherworldly Encounters
Evidence of UFO Sightings and Abductions
NOMAR SLEVIK

Explore the realm of the unknown with more than three dozen true stories of unexplained phenomena. Join ufologist and paranormal researcher Nomar Slevik as he shares fascinating tales of sightings and abductions centered in the Northeast's UFO hotspots. Discover the truth about lights in the sky and aliens on the ground from firsthand witnesses and experiencers.

Otherworldly Encounters includes investigations of UFOs, crop circles, alien abductions, monsters, extraterrestrial biological entities, balls of light, and more. With reports dating back to the 1800s, this is an in-depth guide to phenomena that have puzzled and frightened witnesses for generations. Using the best technological equipment and immersive investigative techniques, Nomar Slevik has collected shocking evidence that is truly out of this world.

978-0-7387-5715-5, 336 pp., 5¼ x 8   **$17.99**

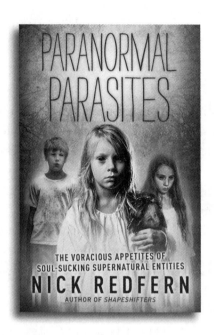

PARANORMAL PARASITES

THE VORACIOUS APPETITES OF
SOUL-SUCKING SUPERNATURAL ENTITIES

NICK REDFERN

AUTHOR OF *SHAPESHIFTERS*

Paranormal Parasites
The Voracious Appetites of Soul-Sucking Supernatural Entities
Nick Redfern

Most people remain oblivious to the truth—there's a monstrous menagerie of supernatural entities that *feed* upon human victims without our knowledge. Fueling themselves with our psychic energy, high states of emotion, and our essential life-force, these dark entities attack as we sleep or even in our waking hours, terrifying and tormenting unsuspecting souls whenever and wherever they can. Join Nick Redfern as he delves deep into the long history of struggle between *us* and *them*. Learn the ways of Shadow People, supernatural seducers, poltergeists, thought-forms, tulpas, the Slenderman, Men in Black, and many other types of energy creatures.

978-0-7387-5355-3, 240 pp., 5¼ x 8   **$16.99**
